Dr. Rhoberta Shaler has worked with hundreds of couples, helping them to save, sustain and strengthen their relationships. She gives them the insights and skills to engage positively and collaboratively, and to disagree or disengage peacefully.

Rather than offer you pages of testimonials from couples who have recaptured their love and re-ignited their passion and commitment, this one recent quote says it all:

"Thank you for helping repair our once great relationship. We both feel strongly it is getting back to where it was because of you."

KAIZEN
for
COUPLES

Smart Steps
to Save, Sustain, and Strengthen
Your Relationship

Rhoberta Shaler, PhD
The Relationship Help Doctor

www.KaizenForCouples.com

Kaizen for Couples:
Smart Steps to Save, Sustain, and Strengthen Your Relationship

Copyright © 2014 Rhoberta Shaler, PhD

Printed in the United States of America

First Edition: First printing, 2014
People Skills Press, San Diego, CA

ISBN: 978-0-9711689-6-1

Editing & cover design by Kera McHugh
somethingelse support studio, www.time4somethingelse.com

Layout & interior design by Maureen Cutajar
Go Published, www.gopublished.com

For information: www.kaizenforcouples.com or 760.747.8686

Dedicated to the courageous couples with whom I have worked—and the couples now looking for answers, insights and skills to deepen their connections—to experience the real joy, deep love and greater intimacy that can be uncovered, recovered, and discovered in their committed relationships. I hope you will continue to take those courageous steps towards each other to create true intimacy, and, to create the sanctuary of a mutual, loving, safe, whole-hearted life together.

Dedicated to my amazing grandchildren, Luka, Mikayla, Anthony, Sofia and Londyn. I hope you will create and enjoy engaging, loving, supportive and mutually-fulfilling relationships throughout your lives.

Acknowledgements

Over the past thirty years, my clients have taught me so much. They invite me into the most intimate aspects of their lives to help them find new paths, moving from long-term pain to recovering and surpassing the love that initially brought them together. That takes courage and willingness. I am grateful for those invitations.

My gratitude for my husband and partner in life, love and learning is endless. He daily inspires me with his brilliance and fearless exploration of possibilities and meaning. He constantly challenges and clarifies my thinking while supporting and loving me unconditionally. I am grateful for his insights, his generosity, his wisdom and his willingness to keep on walking with me, no matter the circumstances.

One of the great assets of my business is Kera McHugh, creator of *somethingelse support studio*. As a highly-skilled web designer, administrator and editor, Kera always has my best interests at heart, and consistently goes the extra mile to make things happen in effective, timely ways. I am grateful for her insights, skills, and generous heart and spirit.

I am grateful for the opportunity to walk with you as you strengthen your relationship.

 Preface

I wrote this book to help you understand the ingredients you need to create the partnership you desire, and hope is possible. That is likely a relationship where you both are known, seen, heard, acknowledged, appreciated and accepted. That may not be how things are working for you right now, but it can become that.

This is the guidebook you need for that journey, especially if any of these issues are currently yours:

- Are you second-guessing your decision to be with your partner?
- Are things rocky right now and you don't have the insights or skills to improve them?
- Do you wonder what to do to make your relationship better?
- Are you afraid you are repeating old patterns in this relationship and you don't know how to step?
- Do you feel torn about wanting your own life AND a partnership?
- Are you living in fear of speaking up, giving up, or walking out?

- Are you frustrated with your partner and don't know where to start to fix things?
- Are you caught between not wanting your partner and not wanting to be alone?
- Do you need a guide and a map to navigating difficulties in your relationship right now?

You may have been attracted to the title because you are currently in a question, in turmoil, in distress or in overwhelm concerning your relationship.
Perfect choice!

I want you to have the insights you need to create the relationship you want…and, likely, with the partner you have right now. You will have the benefit of the four decades of experience I have with helping folks just like you to navigate the difficult patches of life and love. It's not been an easy ride for me, either, so much of what I share with you I've also lived. Deciding to divorce when you have children is difficult. I know because I have done it. Choosing a new partner after disappointment and heartache is scary. Learning to love again can require more trust than you think you have. And, the most important thing I've learned is, with a willing partner, you can indeed see through, think through and work through almost anything and come out on the other side stronger, more aligned, more secure and more in love. I've done that, too!

This book is for you. It offers you a lifeline: the insights, skills, and processes you and your partner can hang on to as you pull yourselves from the treacherous waters and near-drowning experiences of a relationship in trouble to the safety of the boat and the joy of sharing the journey in truth, love and intimacy with your partner. It may also strengthen your own personal lifeline, connecting you to your own truths, your values, vision, beliefs and purpose.

Travel well and keep on walking!

Rhoberta Shaler, PhD
The Relationship Help Doctor

San Diego, CA
July, 2014.

Contents

💕 The Skinny on Relationships

The "skinny" is military slang for the naked, unobscured truth.

T his book could easily begin with feel-goods, rationalizations, and justifications about why you are absolutely right that you deserve to be treated well—and definitely much, much better than you are being treated right now. But it's not going to.

It might also begin with ten things you can do to interest your partner, change your partner or fix your partner. That's not going to happen here, either.

What IS going to happen is that, if you are open, honest and willing, you will take in all that is offered to you here and transform yourself and your relationship in ways that you only hoped for, but were not sure were possible.

You absolutely will find the map for the journey to wholeness, happiness, and real joy. It's up to you whether you use it—or stay where you are!

KAIZEN FOR COUPLES™ is for you if you:

- want to learn how to have a "grown-up relationship"
- are tired of battling, avoiding, ignoring and settling

- are ready and willing to embrace love, trust and intimacy
- know there must be better ways to manage communication, conflict and caring
- want your relationship to work: to grow, strengthen and deepen
- want to feel and know there is one person in your world with whom you are safe in all ways, always
- long to deeply share life and love with your partner, rather than co-exist in a comfortably uncomfortable barter system
- are willing to look at yourself and your partner in new ways in order to have the relationship you want
- are willing to open yourself to the possibility of change: change within yourself AND the relationship in order to have that "grown-up relationship"

The good news is that it all starts with you.

You are always in a relationship. It's that simple. Whether you have a partner, you want a partner, or you are quite happy alone, you are always in a relationship. And, that relationship is reflected in every other relationship you have.

No, this is not a puzzle or a koan. You are always in relationship with yourself, and that is what is reflected in how you see, hear, know, appreciate, acknowledge and accept others. What is going on inside you is the basis for any relationship you have with another person; a parent, a child, a boss, a co-worker, or your life partner.

I know. You would really like to think that any relationship difficulties you are experiencing are caused by someone else's words, behaviors, shortcomings, faults, or, lack of insight and understanding. Your primary relationship would be so much better, you think, if your partner would just "get with the program" or "get his or her act together."

You may have even been to see a relationship expert to get things aired out, fixed, or finished! For many of my clients coming in for their initial visit, the bubble over each of their heads reads:

"Everything in our relationship would be much better
if you would just fix my partner."

Have you ever had that thought? It's common. After all, who wants to start by looking within themselves? It's so much easier to blame, shame, judge and justify!

When problems are "over there" rather than possibly "in here," you can hold on to your drama and your expectations, and make a case that other people will buy about why you *shouldn't* have to put up with this. It makes a great story!

Yes, you may make some appropriate noises about:

"I know it takes two…" or "I am aware I have a part in our issues…"

But, really? Is that whipped cream and window-dressing for this?

"If my partner would stop doing _____, or start doing _____, or not be so self-centered, thoughtless, passive-aggressive, moronic, absorbed, disinterested, lacking in empathy, and/or critical AND grow up, all would be well."

You might even be able to—and no doubt delighted to—add a few things to that list about your partner, right?

Honesty starts right here, so, go ahead and add your beefs right now. Get it out and look at it, no matter how ugly. It's all going on within you and you need to be very honest with yourself. That's the starting point of real change.

The truth is that relationships are ALWAYS in flux. Flux is about two things: the action or process of flowing, and continuous change. And, you were hoping that you could get this relationship nailed down once and for all. Well, that's not going to happen. What can happen, though, is that you can nail the insights, skills, strategies and attitudes that make your journey with your partner honest, trusting, intimate and joyful. Will that be enough for you?

*Relationships are always in flux
and that's healthy.*

Can you think of anything more deadening, stultifying and unexciting than to be with someone who is not changing, not growing, not interested, not curious, not communicative and stuck? Likely not when I put it that way.

One hue and cry that is common when folks come to see me is:
"S/he is not the person I married!"
My response?
"Great. That's very good news."

That's a conversation stopper for a moment or two. The huer and crier was hoping to get agreement that his or her partner not being the person s/he married was a justifiable complaint. It isn't. If you think that your partner is not going to change in response to what life has served up, you think you're in a relationship with a mannequin!

People become interested in new things—hopefully not the neighbor, of course. S/he may have loved kayaking, but now wants to pursue rabbinical studies. S/he may have been naïve and, now that s/he has a few years of living under the belt, has clearer boundaries. Or, perhaps, your partner used to look at you as the source of all wisdom and is now questioning and skeptical.

Change is a reality. Embrace the flux. This is absolutely important to do for your partner...*because you have also changed!*

There is no right model of relationship, barring abuse.

You likely hate being wrong. Most folks do. Perhaps, as a child, you learned that making mistakes or not meeting expectations was unacceptable. Maybe "The Giants" (aka the parents) screamed, scoured or scolded when you did not please them. You quickly learned that there are rules—written and unwritten—about how to keep them happy.

Without some insights—gleaned the hard way, or perhaps through perceptive counseling—you may just still be operating in the "Keeping The Giants Happy" mode. Are you?

Without those insights it's likely you simply swapped "The Giants" for your partner, your boss, or the curious "shoulds" and "should nots" of the culture, the supposed "right" way to do life, like:

- You *should* be ambitious.
- You *should* be focused on success (whatever that is!)
- You *should* have a great relationship with your mother or father.
- You *should* work hard.
- You *should* lose weight.
- You *should* go to college.
- You *should* want expensive things.
- You *should* have a great relationship with your grown children.

- You *should* only say positive things.
- You *should* keep your mouth shut and your opinions to yourself.
- You *should* get married.
- You *should* want to have children.
- You *should* be happy with what you are given.
- You *shouldn't* get "too big for your britches."
- You *shouldn't* want too much.
- You *should* want everything.
- You *should* or *shouldn't* {make up your own}.

"Shoulds" are about obligation, habit, and worst of all, other people's expectations, values and beliefs. They may not suit or serve who you are at this stage of your life, and may not have earlier, either. It's good that you're looking at them right now.

When you live your life thinking you *should* do things a certain way, or have certain goals, you have to be sure they are not limitations, or pie-in-the-sky wish lists. Those result in frustration, unhappiness, and never being content with yourself or others. It all includes that horrible, pervasive idea that you will never be good enough!

"Shoulds" weigh on you terribly. They are heavy, onerous, and often depressing. Whenever you tell yourself, or anyone else, that there is a *should*, you're really expressing or repeating expectations that may or may not have anything to do with what you currently want, feel, believe or need!

Do this exercise:

1. Spend some quiet time writing down all the *shoulds* you've accepted, adopted or inherited. Take enough time to get a hearty list.
2. Reflect on the list: Do you really believe this? Do you really want to live from this list?
3. Release the *shoulds* that no longer serve you. It's very likely you gathered them before you were in charge of your own life. You can let go of them.
4. Replace the *should* with this phrase, "If I really wanted to, I **could**...."
5. Observe the peace that this immediately offers you as you release yourself from the obligations that other people's *shoulds* create!

This simple exercise can shift your thinking in ways that will transform your focus: from being a victim of *shoulds* to being an empowered decision-maker ready to make changes you think are right for you.

A good way to continue this exploration within yourself is to again spend enough quiet time with yourself to answer these questions fully:

- What truly matters to me right now?
- Who do I really believe are people worth taking advice from or being inspired by?
- How do I want to live my life and express my personal values?

Then, do the exercise again this way:

1. What have I been thinking my partner *should* do?
2. How have I been thinking my partner *should* respond, react, or think?
3. Does this allow for seeing my partner as s/he really is?

4. Could I release these *shoulds* that are clouding my vision of my partner?
5. How can I look at my partner with softer eyes and fewer expectations?

Do you see how this can make a big difference in your relationship, quickly?

That's the beginning of KAIZEN FOR COUPLES: taking a positive step towards your partner in your mind, and demonstrating that step by the way you interact with him or her right away.

There is no one ideal kind of relationship.

You and your partner likely come from somewhat different systems: different families, different beliefs, different expectations, different rules, different ideas of what is right, wrong, good or bad. You are simply not the same. Yet, there is some idea that the ideal is to *be* on the same page, singing from the same sheet of music at the same time, all the time. Let that go!

Relationships are in flux because people are in flux. You change. You change your mind, your plans, your hair, your underwear. These changes are neither right nor wrong. They are just next.

The way other people do their relationships may have little or no application to creating the best relationship for you two. Others will be happy to tell you what you *should* do. You know that. But, don't let them *should* on you! **This is your relationship, not theirs. That's why I highly recommend that you only discuss your relationship with your partner and your therapist. No one else.**

When your relationship becomes a topic of conversation with family and friends, don't be surprised if they flood you with conflicting opinions, edicts and "what-ifs." They will. They may be trying to be helpful. But, it's not often useful. It can destroy your relationship, too, because each person will feel that, if you adopt what they suggest, you are saying they are right. The converse is also true: you don't do what they suggest and you've made them wrong. Remember earlier in this chapter: People do not like being wrong. So, do the math: you can lose people from your life because you don't take their relationship advice, or you can lose them because you do take their advice. It's much wiser to simply not give them the chance to offer it!

Discussing your relationship with anyone beyond your partner and therapist can create alienation. In the worst case scenario, you just want to tell someone how you really feel so you spill it all in unfiltered language to your best friend. Your best friend now thinks your partner is a miserable so-and-so with no right to treat you in those ways. Next time your best friend sees your partner, it is likely there will be a different reception. And, you set it up. You may well be over the upset with your partner, but the story lives on in your best friend's head and is highly likely to be told repeatedly. Not a good scenario. Convinced now? Only talk with your partner and your therapist!

Are you flexible and resilient enough to entertain and accept change—the condition Epictetus called the only permanent thing in life? Or, are you clinging onto the way it is supposed to be? The only right way? The way "they" told you it would be? The way it used to be? Those are recipes for discontent, disappointment and difficulties. If you are experiencing relationship issues right now, it is likely that those things are part of the distressing mix.

There is no ideal relationship, only the one you consciously sculpt together, the one that works for both of you and keeps you growing in safe, respectful, trusting ways. That's the one that allows for true emotional intimacy.

There is no one to blame for your happiness or unhappiness. Darn! There's no one to blame? But, it's so convenient to blame your partner for all that is wrong in your world. Then, you move onto another lethal game: the "if only" game. You know it. It sounds like this:

> "If only my partner cared more, I would be happier."

> "If only my partner cleaned up after him/herself, there would be less friction."

> "If only my partner made more money, I wouldn't be so anxious."

> "If only my partner was more interested in sex, I would be more interested in him/her."

What are your "if onlys?"

> "If only my partner would _____, then I would feel or be _____."

Unless you are a saint, you have at least one or two. You may never have said them out loud, but they are in there, rattling around in your head.

Time to take back ownership of your own life and not decide how you feel based on what someone else did, does, says or said. You are in charge, and hopefully you'll take control of how you feel. It is your chosen response to any situation, maybe not in the exact moment, but on quiet reflection. You'll learn how to do this with much greater ease and grace by using the *Personal Weather Report* you'll learn in this book.

Let me clarify that reflective practice further:

- Someone says something that hurts you.
- You say "Ouch."

- You sit with and think about why it hurt you.
- You decide that a) it is unnecessary to feel hurt about it because it was information about the other person, not really about you, or b) you recognize that what s/he said is accurate or inaccurate.
- You assess your response based on your own values, vision and beliefs about your life.
- Now, you are nearer to knowing yourself better and living more authentically in alignment with your values, vision, beliefs and purposes.

No one is responsible for, or accountable for, your happiness. That's an inside job. Once you have the Relational Gifts™ in alignment within you, then you will have them to give. You'll learn more about those in the chapter, "Do You Have These Gifts To Give?" Until then, work on that inside job!

ALL relationships come complete with hurts, pains, difficulties and complications. It's just a matter of degree.

It would be unwise to expect that relationships are a breeze, and that both parties love, appreciate, agree with and otherwise delight each other at all times. That doesn't happen. However, I have worked with couples who go through The Wedding Daze absolutely convinced that marriage will be heaven: collaborative, cooperative, loving, trusting, intimate…and EASY.

For the last year or so, I have been working with a young couple who started out as best friends, moved into a relationship, very quickly got engaged and headed straight into The Wedding Daze. That's the state in which the wedding is all the focus and the relationship, not so much.

Although I suggested a "once-around-the-sun" engagement as I do with all my couples, they simply could not see any wisdom in that. Being engaged for a whole year before having a wedding seemed a waste of time to them. They soon learned that I was wiser than they thought. In my experience, once the idea of a long-term committed relationship has been accepted by both partners, there is so much to learn about yourself and each other...*before the wedding or co-habiting.*

Just making such a major commitment is an incredible emotional shift that takes time to settle in. Realizing that this is the last person you are ever going to kiss, hold and be intimate with is big. Then, knowing that this is the person you are going to love, live and grow with for a long time takes accepting.

Why is it such a good idea to wait a year before marrying or moving in together? Because you have to assimilate the emotional shifts while working out the communication, conflict management and differences in temperament, personality, allegiances, and even logistics. Now it makes sense, right?

The Hokey-Pokey Relationship

So recently, this newly-married young couple asked for a relationship session because things had hit the rocks once again. And, the old telltale signs of a "one foot in and one foot out" relationship—the hokey-pokey kind of relationship—shot to the surface and spilled out of their mouths:

"I just cannot do this anymore. I'm just done!"

"I just don't find her as attractive as I used to."

"I shouldn't have to put up with this stuff."

"This is not what I signed up for."

"He's just too immature and it's not changing."

These days, many couples start their supposedly committed relationships with conditionally committed behaviors and mindsets. They seem to think that it is all going to come together effortlessly, and that marriage or co-habitation seals that deal. They are not committed to the process, and may not be as committed to the person as would be optimal, either.

When you're in a relationship for what you can get out of it, you're in trouble. That's what a "one foot in and one foot out" relationship is. They are simply not "All in!"

> *"They put one foot in and leave one foot out.*
> *They do the hokey-pokey and they turn themselves around.*
> *And that's WHAT IT'S ALL ABOUT!"*

They are not really committed to each other nor are they committed to the relationship, building it by walking through whatever hurts, pains, fears, expectations, difficulties and complications come along. They want it all to happen organically in some no-work, easy-breezy way. And, there is a reason for that—not a good one, but a reason.

> *They go into it thinking:*
> *"I can always get a divorce if it doesn't work out."*

Yes, that's true, you can.
Yes, that's the kiss of death to a commitment.
In fact, it is NOT a commitment at all!

Once the idea that you can get a divorce at any time permeates your relationship, you stop being committed to finding solutions and are more likely to issue ultimatums. It is so common that it is a main contributor to the high divorce rate.

If s/he doesn't:

- please me
- do what I want
- meet my needs or demands
- stop doing what irritates me
- change his/her ways
- desire sex when I want it
- like all my friends
- put my needs first
- think my way
- cater to my whims, desires, and wants

…then, I'm outta here.

Anything sounding familiar from your friends…or, maybe from your mouth?

Harsh news: Those are extremely immature conditions for a committed relationship. Emotional grownups do not have this list. Petulant children do. No wonder the divorce rate is high!

Relationships are going to be just like life:
painful, difficult and complicated.

Love and commitment do not end that. Love simply gives you a partner to work life through with, to walk with through all the ups, downs and side ways of life, and of life together. Love strengthens when you can truly offer each other the Relational Gifts.

The principles and insights in KAIZEN FOR COUPLES give you the tools and skills you need to solve problems, not suffer from them.

Using the RelationSteps™ and The Relationship Kaizen Convercycle™ in this book, you'll find clear ways to create the relationship you most want—a grown-up relationship.

Keep reading, but only if you actually want an emotionally mature, emotionally intimate relationship based on truth, trust and intimacy, a relationship that will only keep getting better as you walk together. That is a truly loving relationship.

CHAPTER 2

❤️ Perhaps Love...

The word *"love"* is used in so many ways, in so many contexts, by so many people. What does it actually mean to you? You might say that you love your mother, your dog, your home, or even a new paint color. What does it mean?

Love is something you cannot capture. You cannot possess it. You cannot keep it in a box. You cannot control it.

Love is an experience. And, it is different for each person. There are no rules, no checklists, no scorecards. There is no one right way to experience it, or to recognize it. It is elusive. Yet, you think you know it when you feel it. Curious, isn't it?

When John Denver wrote the song, *Perhaps Love*, he captured the essence of its elusiveness:

> Perhaps love is like a resting place
> A shelter from the storm
> It exists to give you comfort
> It is there to keep you warm
> And in those times of trouble

When you are most alone
The memory of love will bring you home.

Perhaps love is like a window
Perhaps an open door
It invites you to come close
It wants to show you more
And even if you lose yourself
And don't know what to do
The memory of love will see you through.

Oh, love to some is like a cloud
To some as strong as steel
For some a way of living
For some a way to feel
And some say love is holding on
And some say letting go
And some say love is everything

And some say they don't know.
Perhaps love is like the ocean
Full of conflict, full of pain
Like a fire when it's cold outside
Or thunder when it rains
If I should live forever
And all my dreams come true
My memories of love will be of you[1]

---

[1] Denver, John. Cherry Lane Music Publishing Company, Inc. (ASCAP) © 1980.

So, perhaps love is what you make it, what you remember, what you feel. Or, maybe it scares you because you have unmet expectations of receiving it from your parents, or someone else you looked to for it.

There are no rules for love. Love simply realizes itself in the now, at this time, in this heart, in this way.

Perhaps love is an onion you have to unpeel.
It brings a lot of tears but it adds so much
to the flavor of your life.

You have to set aside how it's "supposed" to look and feel. You have to set aside the abstractions and choose to live love. You can know it. You can experience it, but you cannot justify or validate it. That's where it often comes into conflict with the moral universe.

People love rules because they give them something to measure things against. They can easily see black and white, right and wrong, good and bad. They have their ruler to measure rightness and think that it gives them the right to judge. I disagree. There is no right way that love is "supposed" to look, feel and be—except non-violent.

Love is a feeling. Love is actions. Love is communication. Love is an experience. Can you actually have rules for that?

This whole idea of what love *should* look, feel, sound and be like is a set-up for blame, shame, judgment and justification. In fact, that's why love often turns into a barter system, an exchange that comes complete with scorecard! Who did what to whom? When? For how long? Who owes who? Who's paying back whom?

Some authors, like Gary Chapman with *The Five Languages of Love*,[2] try to help couples understand how to deepen their relationship by attuning to what each partner recognizes as love. It certainly can help. It also can set up a kind of barter system, another scoreboard to keep track of points gained and lost. Not a good idea at all, then.

Although you can defend it because it can be seen as a gift you can give to your partner when you know what looks and feels like love to him or her, it also sets up the possibility of withholding the very thing from him or her that you know is wanted when you are not feeling loving towards them. A double-edged sword, for sure!

> *Love is not about getting.*
> *Love is about forgetting.*

What do you have to forget? The balance sheet, the scoreboard, the gamesmanship, and often yourself. All barter dynamics in contemporary relationships have nothing to do with love. They have to do with self-satisfaction. That old radio station, WIIFM: What's In It For Me. That makes love about you. Is that what it is about?

Love is experienced in the flow. It doesn't just give you what you need or want. It just gives. You have all the flow you allow.

Sometimes, you think you have some supposedly legitimate expectations which are, in reality, cleverly constructed ego traps. You think you have the right to expect certain things from life, and in the same way, from your partner "if s/he really loves you."

---

[2] Chapman, Gary. The Five Love Languages: How to Express Heartfelt Commitment to Your Mate, Northfield Press, 2004.

Bridget came to see me to hopefully find out why she was so unhappy and unsatisfied most of the time and to discover what would make her happy. We had been working on it for a few weeks, and as she was leaving one session, I told her I hoped she would make it a good week. She said,

"I will. It's my birthday on Tuesday."

"Great. How will you celebrate?"

"Ideally, **he** will remember. He'll bring me flowers and take me out to a fancy restaurant for dinner. And, he'll bring me a gift that is personal and has nothing to do with the house."

"Did you tell him what you want?"

"No, of course not. (Watch out. Here it comes!) **If he really loves me, he'll know what I want.**"

(That is a killer statement. If you've ever said or even thought it, stop now!)

"Do you love your husband, Bridget?"

"Yes, I do."

"Then, why wouldn't you tell him what you want so that he can do exactly what would please you the most? Why do you want him to prove to you that he is a mind reader?"

Then, she said it again!

"If he really loves me, he'll know what I want."

"Well, in my opinion, if you don't tell him what would make you happy, you're setting yourself up for an unhappy birthday, and you're setting your husband up for being wrong. There's no love in that."

Bridget went on her way. You won't be surprised to learn that, on her return the next week, she had a story about her birthday.

"He remembered my birthday and he brought me flowers. When I opened his gift, it was an electric fry pan and he asked me what was for dinner!"

And, she was not a happy camper at all!

"You didn't tell him what you wanted, did you?" And she said it again,

"If he really loved me, he would have figured it out."

"Sorry to say, Bridget, but you got the birthday you wanted. You set it up this way and you asked for it."

Again, she was not a happy camper. She did not want to accept any responsibility for setting her husband up to fail. She could not see how unloving this supposed "test" of his love was, unloving to her husband and unloving to herself.

Can you see it? I hope so. No one can read your mind. No one can be expected to read your mind. You cannot read your partner's mind, or your mother's mind, or your child's mind. That's why love is found in communication!

Bridget denied it. Will you accept it?

Denial is a closed system.
Love must be an open system.

Denial is a closed system. Genuine, authentic love is an open system. A closed system is one which doesn't exchange anything with anything or anyone in its surroundings. An open system is the opposite: it is continually interacting with its environment or surroundings. Love must be an open system.

Love in interactive. It is found in the exchanges of looks, words, thoughts, visions, beliefs and actions. Love interacts with its environment and flows. Bridget wanted her husband to demonstrate that he really knew who she was and what she liked and wanted. She tested him. In doing so, they both lost a beautiful opportunity to celebrate their love. And, Bridget set it up that way.

Love is interactive. You trust enough to gently open up your innermost thoughts and feelings with each other. You trust that your tender feelings, fears and desires will be treated with respect. You feel loved when that happens. You feel devastated when it doesn't.

Love is not so much a feeling as it is an energy.
And, energy flows.

Love flows from you. Love flows to you. You are in charge of what flows from you. That's all!

Love needs to be "realized": it needs to be made so. Only you can do that for yourself. If love isn't realized, it is not love.

Love can flow from you in all directions, to all people. Or, love can be focused on your partner. And, you can do both and much more at the same time. That's because there are different kinds of love. Although recent writers have suggested there are up to fifteen kinds of love, there are basically four kinds of love that historically happen to come from Greek terms. These are *agape, eros, phillia* and *storge* and they are very different from each other. It's worth knowing these differences so that you can actually distinguish what you are feeling for another person, or in a particular relationship or situation.

- **Agape** – This is selfless love that gives and expects nothing in return. It is love in the spiritual sense, accepting and loving regardless of return or conditions. Thomas Aquinas, following Aristotle, described love as "to will the good of another."
- **Eros** – This is the physical passionate love that goes along with sensual love and desire. It is romantic without any balancing elements such as logic, reason or rationale. It is that chemistry that draws us to a potential mate and leads us to commit to that person. Love at first sight falls into this category, too. It is what we call "intimate love."
- **Phillia** – This a general decision to love and means extending affectionate regard or friendship to others. It is both give and take and generally includes loyalty to your family, friends and community. It requires equality and familiarity, so it also extends somewhat into that which lovers feel.
- **Storge** – This is really natural affection combined with acceptance. Usually it is used to describe that kind of love where you love someone but don't necessarily like everything about them, so there is a degree of "putting up with" things, often within the family.

All of these different expressions of love, different depths of love, are within our understanding of love. And, you need some of each to have a healthy, mutual, empathetic, vital relationship with your partner!

Not all relationships are mutual. That not only means that not all relationships have love flowing back and forth, but that it is unwise to even expect them to be equitable all the time. Think of the relationship parents have with their children. They pour love into their children (in the best of times) and, if the parents are mature grown-ups, they are not expecting that they are going to get all that love back. They give their children opportunities and material things, and they do not expect reciprocity. You pour into your children all your gifts so that they will, in turn, pour them into their children. That water runs downstream. It is supposed to. It is not recycled. Expecting it to return in the same way is setting yourself up for heartache. It's lovely when it returns, and still lovely when it pours forth, without return.

Your partnership with your chosen one is not like that.

Couples love has to be mutual, otherwise, it denigrates into a game of tit-for-tat, shame, blame, games and manipulations.

Not a pretty picture to look at, and a horrible ride to take. And, neither are necessary.

Love is not an obligation or a duty.
Love is not abusive, or accepting of abuse.
Love is freedom and power.
Love is an abstraction, but loving isn't.
Love is a choice.

So, perhaps love?

CHAPTER 3

What is Kaizen For Couples?

Y ou want your relationship to be great: loving, honest, trusting, intimate, supportive, reciprocal and fun. And, you have times like that or else you would not have stayed in the relationship. You love your partner, or at least, you love some things about your partner. There are a few things—or a whole lot of things—that could improve and that is why you chose this book.

When things go sideways, or very, very wrong in your relationship, you want them to change. You want them fixed, and you want them fixed NOW! You want the pain, fear, frustration and stress to stop.

You would like to be able to fix the big issues in your relationship in one fell swoop. In fact, you may even think that that is supposed to be possible. You learned it well from sweeping admonitions from a parent:

"You better straighten up!"

"Clean up your act!"

"Get better grades!"

"Be more considerate."

Wow! Did you have any idea how to do those huge undertakings when you heard those words? Likely not. And, it seemed daunting, scary and fraught with the ability to fail!

Now that you're grown, that's still lurking in your subconscious. So, it is no wonder that partners making requests for change from you cause you to become fearful and get your back up a little. You might have no idea where to go with it, just as you had no idea what your parent really wanted from you. Your response in your head, at least, might sound like this:

"How dare you tell me what to do! Who do you think you are?"

"Are you saying I'm not competent, or worse, that I am wrong?"

"Oh, there it is goes again. I cannot do anything right."

"I just will never be good enough."

"This isn't what I thought love or marriage would be like. I thought I'd have one person who wasn't always picking me apart or making demands I don't know how to fulfill."

"I don't want someone else telling me how to be!"

Those things above that might run through your head are big, big concepts that cover a lot of territory. KAIZEN FOR COUPLES is your next best step. You need to break those next steps into doable, small pieces.

Broad strokes—coming at you or coming from within you—leave you wondering where to start, what to do, and how to know if you have done whatever is requested soon enough, often enough, or well enough. For many, that's too much to undertake or figure out, so you just keep doing what you're doing, hoping for the best. You feel disempowered, yet you'd like to improve. That's where Kaizen comes in.

Kaizen is such a beautiful word. It is simple, crisp and optimally descriptive of the very best ways for you to approach everything in your world. It is the optimal way to approach your relationships, for sure!

Kaizen is a combination of two Japanese words that replace this sentence:

Consistently taking small incremental steps that make sustainable positive improvements.

That's a lot to say. The Japanese eloquently shorten all that to the word, Kaizen. It is comprised of two Japanese words, *kai* which means "change", and *zen* which means "good." So, simply "good change," change that moves you in a positive direction, closer to clarity, love, respect, and to one another.

You want to steadily move forward in small ways that consistently improve your relationship with your partner. You want to know there are effective steps you can take, now and in the future, that will always keep you moving towards the greater truth, trust and emotional intimacy that are at the heart of love.

You want reliable steps you can return to again and again. You want to know what those steps are, and how to take them together, effectively, consistently and joyfully. KAIZEN FOR COUPLES shows you the ways.

"Kaizen" was the name given to the total quality management system begun by William Edwards Deming.

> "He was a visionary, whose tireless quest for the truth and unwavering belief in continual improvement led to a set of transformational theories and teachings that changed the way we think about quality, management and leadership. Throughout his career, he remained a gentleman devoted to family, supportive of colleagues and friends, and always true to his word and beliefs."[3]

Deming turned manufacturing—and management—on its ear with his innovative approaches. So ahead of his time, he had to leave the United States in order to find a culture open to his innovations. He found that in the Toyota Corporation in Japan. His systems and philosophies have influenced thousands of companies and executives to find the pathways to excellence for their people, products and profits.

> *"It is not enough to do your best;*
> *you must know what to do,*
> *and then do your best."*
> *— W. Edwards Deming*

What Deming created for business has powerful applications for your life, your health, your career, *and* your relationships. That's the basis of KAIZEN FOR COUPLES. Following Kaizen principles, couples systematically choose to make small positive incremental improvements continuously. That may mean working with a new skill or insight that makes sense to you both for a best next step. You'll find many of those as you read through the book.

---

[3] About W. Edwards Deming. www.Deming.org 2014.

Kaizen is gentle. It is important that the steps you take together are small, sometimes tiny. The key is to choose steps that are "doable." In my book, *Prevent Free Fall: Pack Your Own Parachute*,[4] I talk about the value of breaking projects or tasks down into "teeny, tiny doable chunks." I call those "TTDCs." Whether you are renovating your kitchen, your health, or your relationship, it is wise to keep that focus: one small TTDC at a time!

KAIZEN FOR COUPLES invites you to enhance your ability to talk productively together. That might seem strange to use the word 'productively' in terms of a conversation with your partner, but it's appropriate. You want your conversations to lead somewhere, to create a change, deepen your understanding, gain an insight. What you don't want is conversations to turn into confrontations that lead to conflagrations!

KAIZEN FOR COUPLES will help you have productive conversations that lead to more truth, trust and emotional intimacy. The key is willingness, real boots-on-the-ground, roll-up-your-sleeves willingness.

WHERE ARE YOU?

Able Willing	Unable Willing
Able Unwilling	Unable Unwilling

---

[4] Shaler, Rhoberta. *Prevent Free Fall: Pack Your Own Parachute*. People Skills Press. 2006.

"Able" means that you know how to do something.

"Willing" means that you want to do something.

Can you see how this can really help you identify your starting point in any difficult conversation, especially when you are grappling with a troubling issue? Noting your basic, underlying ability or willingness is key to solving a problem, getting something done, and knowing where your resistances are. That's why this is a very helpful chart.

The primary questions for each partner in the relationship are:

Am I able?
Am I willing?

- Do you know how to communicate with your partner?
- Do you know how to successfully manage conflicts?
- Do you know how to talk through issues without anger, demands, threats or ultimatums?
- Do you know how to negotiate respectfully?
- Are you willing to learn the skills you need to have the abilities you know would positively affect your relationship?
- Are you willing to set aside your reluctance to talk about difficult things?
- Are you willing to put the past behind you and create a new future together?
- Are you willing to work things through even if the progress is slow?
- Are you willing to treat your partner in honest, respectful ways?

WHAT IS KAIZEN FOR COUPLES?

These are basic questions that need only one answer: yes!

If that is not the answer from each of you, there really is no willingness to enhance, improve or restore your relationship. It all does come down to willingness.

If you are willing, and you put in the time, energy and effort, KAIZEN FOR COUPLES will work for you. You'll feel empowered, encouraged and energized knowing that you and your partner can see through, think through and work through any issues that come up between you. Your confidence as a team will heighten your sense of true partnership. What a great result!

💕 What Could Possibly Go Wrong?

You need to be safe to discuss any topic with your partner.

I n a committed relationship, you need to be committed to conscious communication. You want to create a safe atmosphere where anything can be discussed at any time. Does that sound like a tall order?

Can you currently bring up any topic, any issues, without fear of withholding, anger or shut-down? Are you available to each other to know, see, hear and acknowledge what is true for each other, without immediately relating it to yourself and becoming defensive? If not, that is your first step in working the KAIZEN FOR COUPLES principles.

Earlier, I mentioned that you took in a lot of your ways of being in relationship from your early life. Parents may have made those sweeping generalized sentences like "Clean up your act." and you had no idea how to do that, what it meant or where to begin. It was overwhelming and defeating. Then, your partner says something like: "If you can't treat me with more respect, I'm out of here." It triggers the same fear of not knowing and not being able to match up to the challenge that the first did when you were a child. You are not thinking about those earlier demands, but your subconscious registers it. And, you become defensive.

Defensiveness is not the same thing as defending yourself.

Defending yourself is a response to **a real threat** to your personal safety whether that is a physical attack, an attack on your **character, or an attack against your ideas or beliefs.**

Defensiveness, on the other hand, is a response that is coming **from a perceived–or imagined or assumed–threat** or attack on your sense of yourself.

Defensiveness is a psychological response. The threat, demand or statement you are reacting or responding to may be striking a chord within you that you didn't even know was being played. It's likely not coming even from your current relationship. It is a deep response that lets you know that you have a few old fears and patterns that would be good to investigate with the help of a professional. Otherwise, defensiveness holds you back from learning about yourself and your partner.

If you were being literally attacked, a reasonable response would be to defend and protect yourself, or your decisions, ideas and character. If you are being accused of something you didn't do, you can bring up evidence to show that you are not to blame. That is an example of an appropriate time to defend.

Defensiveness arises when your own sense of yourself, of who you are, *feels* like it is being attacked. Your reptilian brain senses danger, a threat to your survival. It's almost instinctive, it happens so quickly and without much conscious effort. And, it often is simply not accurate!

The supposed attacker may have had no intention of attack, and may well deny the attack–but you can *feel* attacked nonetheless. Often, it arises because you previously experienced an actual attack (verbal or otherwise) that left an indelible emotional mark on you, and was intended to be hurtful. You have to have the wisdom to separate out what was going on in your past from what is occurring right now in your current relationship!

Most often, defensiveness pushes other people away. It severs your connection with your partner because it is simply not warranted and seldom results in improving your relationship. Defensiveness shows that you are more concerned with protecting yourself than with creating a deeper connection with your partner. It triggers an internal experience that may have been lingering around for a long time.

When you become defensive in a conversation with your partner, it often leads to a distancing between you. This is neither good nor necessary. Note that the stronger your sense of self, the less likely you are to become defensive. Often my clients find that the more work we undertake individually on these issues, the closer they can become with their partners. Win-win, for sure! So, there is a way to turn defensiveness around.

Imagine how it would change things if, at the moment you feel defensive, you were able to flip a switch within that would allow you to become more concerned with learning about your partner than with responding defensively. That could really change things for the good.

What if, in the first moment you felt defensive, you were able to remember:

> "This person is my partner, my love, my friend. I'm going to learn more about what s/he is thinking rather than respond from my fears."

Can you imagine that that would be a major shift for you, and for the relationship?

When you first notice that defensiveness is rising in you, you could even begin by telling your partner about your internal process. It might sounds like this:

> "I can hear and see that you are upset with me (or about me or something I said or did) and I am feeling attacked right now. That may not be your intention and I want to share with you where I'm at with it right now."

Wouldn't that have an amazing effect on the conversation? It carries the potential for slowing that conversation down, and learning more about each other. It can mean all the difference between escalation and alienation, insight and closeness. Being able to say that is a kaizen step, a valuable good change. It is a small step in a positive direction towards what you most want: a close, loving, respectful relationship.

You can replace defensiveness with a few far more engaging steps that can really help your relationship:

1. Notice where you are feeling defensive and say so, taking responsibility for that feeling rather than blaming your partner.

2. Just ask. "Were you attacking or accusing me intentionally?"

3. Check in with your partner. Ask if s/he is upset with you at this time. Assumptions destroy communication.

4. Stop and ask yourself if the current conversation or situation reminds you of other times when you felt similarly. Isolate the earliest times and see what you learn by doing that yourself.

5. Ask yourself: "Is it the words, the tone of voice, the subject matter or just the way that I'm feeling today that is making me respond defensively?"

6. If you are feeling unfairly blamed or accused, say so. It's enough to say so without adding your own accusations or blame to the situation: "Regardless of your intent, I am feeling accused."

7. Have a conversation, not a fight.

Use these thoughts above to turn your conflict into communication!

CHAPTER 5

Do You Have the Gifts to Give?

It is impossible to give a gift you do not have.

When you do try to give a gift you do not have in your possession, it leads to resentment. Think of this scenario:

You have a friend who is going through a rough time. She really needs someone to talk to and someone to help out with the things she doesn't have the energy to do. You step up to be that someone because you care about her.

Time passes and you start to feel a little irked each time she calls, or asks for something. You beat yourself up when you feel that because you wonder what kind of a friend are you if you can't help out willingly and freely.

It goes on. Now, you are not just irked, but slipping quickly into full-blown resentment. Doesn't she know you have a life, too?

What's going on here is so common: you are trying to give a gift you don't have. In this case, you are trying to give her the time, energy, support, presence and grace that you do not give to yourself!

That's a bit like buying something on your credit card. You really cannot afford it or you would pay cash, but you buy it anyway. You are enjoying it so much. Then, the bill comes and you still don't have the cash. You pay a little but you're still enjoying what you bought, so it's worth it. Then, another bill comes along with the credit charges. Oooh! That's a bit of a reality check. You pay a portion and drift along for another month. Still can't pay it off. More credit charges. Now what you bought is not seeming so wise...or, enjoyable. You begin to resent the charges, the credit card company, the financial system, the economy and even your partner!

That's like trying to give a gift you don't have. You cannot do it for very long and you soon begin to resent being asked to try.

RELATIONAL GIFTS

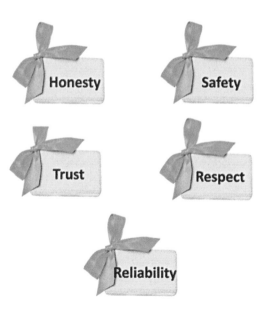

The basis for a healthy relationship with yourself and anyone else is found in the Relational Gifts. The two fundamental questions are:

Do you give them to yourself?
Do you have them to give?

If you are not scrupulously honest with yourself, you cannot be honest with others. It's not possible. You cannot give a gift you do not have! The same goes for the other four gifts. If you don't keep your promises to yourself, you cannot trust yourself. If you don't keep your promises to others, you are unreliable.

Let's talk about trust. An obvious example is a New Year's Resolution, or a decision to exercise. You decide what you want and what you will do to achieve it. You start. Do well. Slack off and quit. Can you now trust yourself to fulfill your commitments to yourself? No. You just told yourself that you are unimportant. It sounds harsh, but it's accurate. You may never have thought about it at this level before.

Honesty

Ever since someone coined the phrase that became popular in the 1980s, "Denial is not a river in Egypt," we have keenly recognized the possibility of being dishonest with ourselves. It's clever, cryptic and ac-curate. People struggling with addictions often have addiction to denial as well. Giving up denial would mean recognizing any need for change. Similarly, it is so easy for people to turn a blind eye to what prevents them from being honest with themselves. That sounds like a contradic-tion but think of it in terms of this common example:

Dan is a functioning alcoholic. He goes to work, often hung over, but gets there and does an adequate job. When his wife and family try to talk to him about his drinking, in particular about how they miss him when he simply "disappears" after he's had a few drinks in the evening, he denies he has a drinking problem. He uses the fact that he goes to work every day and stays home most nights as evidence that he is fully-functioning and responsible. Therefore, he has no problem. That's denial.

Denial is the refusal to accept reality or fact, acting instead as though a painful event, thought or feeling simply does not exist. It is a psychologically primitive defense mechanism, employed to avoid dealing with painful feelings or areas of life you don't want to think about or admit. Here's another example:

> Gwen has been diagnosed with colon cancer, discovered incidentally during a CT scan ordered for another possible condition. During the initial workup to further investigate the cancer, several spots were seen on her lung. She focused on getting rid of the colon cancer through extensive surgery and minimal chemotherapy, sure that would take care of the problem. Over the eighteen months of dealing with colon issues, she steadfastly refused to see a pulmonary specialist regarding her lungs. She denies there could be anything further that needs attention. It is likely her fear that feeds her denial.

Denial is the outright refusal to admit or recognize that something has occurred or is currently occurring. You don't have to be self-destructive to be in denial!

Denial is the antithesis of honesty. When things are not going well in your relationship, you may make excuses for it.

> "She's really jealous but it's only because she loves him so much."

"He's having difficulties at work and that is what is causing him to be so distant."

"My daughter is getting really thin, but there's nothing wrong with wanting to look like a model, is there?"

"He's under a lot of pressure to succeed, so what's wrong with a few drinks to take the pressure off in the evenings."

Denial goes right along with two other defense mechanisms you might recognize: **minimization** which admits the fact but denies their seriousness, and **projection** which admits both the fact and the seriousness but denies responsibility by blaming somebody or something else.

If you are in denial that your relationship is declining, or stalled in neutral, you are missing out on the positive possibilities for your life together. And, if you are not being honest with yourself, you cannot be honest with anyone else. It's just not possible.

The flip side of denial is honesty. It is being truthful and sincere. It is without deceit, fraud or diversion. It is coming to terms with what you really think, what is really going on and who you really are.

And, beware of thinking that you are "saving yourself or someone from the truth" with dishonesty or omission. Sure, you can safely distract or divert attention from the truth when someone asks you if s/he looks fat in those jeans. But, any aware person recognizes the dodge and knows the truth anyway. Being honest does not have to be brutal. In fact, I would like to strangle the person who created the phrase "brutal honesty." It is entirely possible to be totally kind and totally honest at the same time. It just takes practice.

To be honest with your partner, you must be honest with yourself—kindly, totally honest.

Safety

Are you safe with you? Along with telling yourself the truth, do you keep yourself safe?

Keeping yourself safe means being able to express clear boundaries and maintain them. Do you recognize toxic situations and people? That's where you need those boundaries.

In common usage, a boundary is a line that separates one thing from another, like the wall of a house, or a fence. That's how psychological boundaries act, too. They separate the private side of life from the public side. A boundary separates our relationship and what goes on inside it from what other people have access to. It is a safe place for emotional intimacy.

If one partner shares intimate details of the relationship with others outside the relationship, the boundary fails and safety is lost. That is why I make every effort with the couples I work with to have them understand why it is important to agree to only share details of their relationship with each other and me, and no one else. It is because of the safety of boundaries.

(Remember from earlier that everyone else you might consider close enough to share details of your relationship with has a vested interest and an allegiance, as well as an opinion about what you "should" do. They are unlikely to provide you with a neutral, supportive ear and professionally helpful insights.)

Psychological boundaries help you, as an individual, to define yourself, your values, your vision, your beliefs and how you want to be treated. When you are clear on those things and can express that clarity to your partner, you are creating emotional intimacy. When those boundaries are maintained, you will both know how to treat one another with respect, how to care for each other, and, importantly, how not to take one another for granted. When they are not maintained, when one partner abuses the other in any way— even by making unilateral decisions that affect you both, resentment grows.

Boundary violations are big issues in many relationships. If one partner causes the other to feel belittled, unimportant, or in any way abused, it may cause the other partner to learn how best to defend him/herself. When that happens, there is no safety.

To maintain your own safety in the world, you have to learn how to interact with intrusive or abusive people in ways that will make them respect your boundaries, back off, or leave you alone. However, you must learn how to recognize and become aware that you are actually being violated and intruded upon in the first place.

You are in charge of your safety. You must become firm in your conviction that you are worthy, and certainly deserve to be treated well. That's what becoming an assertive, not aggressive, person is all about. Take it to heart. It will keep you safe.

If you need help to establish and express your boundaries, get it now. It will make a huge difference in your quality of life, and it can change your relationships significantly. And, those changes will be for the better in any case. Trust me.

Trust

You know how big an issue trust is. If you've ever been betrayed, you really know. It becomes a very sensitive area for you that can permeate every relationship.

Do you trust yourself?
Can you count on yourself?
Do you keep your promises to yourself?
Do you trust that you have what it takes no matter what life presents?

You come by your unwillingness to trust yourself very honestly. If you are like most children, you were told what to do, what to think, what to value and how to behave. You have spent your life listening to others: parents, teachers, pastors, managers, leaders. You might choose what you have been told to choose. You were told who you are and who you *should* be. You molded yourself to the feedback others gave you about what was good, bad, and good enough. You sought approval and reached for recognition and acceptance.

In a healthy world, it makes sense to learn from the experiences and wisdom of others, to rely on their learning and follow their lead. The world and its inhabitants are not always healthy and the learning is not always helpful. And, there is a high cost that often is extracted in your adult life: you get in the habit of shaping yourself to the desires, preferences and expectations of others. In doing that, you risk losing yourself. And, you lose—or fail to develop—the ability to trust yourself! In the worst cases, you freeze without their direction. You are unable to make decisions and choices because you lack trust in your own insights and inner knowing.

In an article in the Harvard Business Review, Peter Bregman shared this poem by David Wagoner, *The Hero with One Face*, and his thoughts on it:

> I chose what I was told to choose:
> They told me gently who I was...
> I wait, and wonder what to learn...
> O here, twice blind at being born.

Bregnan says, "There is a simple remedy to the insecurity of being ourselves: stop asking.

Instead, take the time, and the quiet, to decide what you think. That is how we find the part of ourselves we gave up. That is how we become powerful, clever, creative, and insightful. That is how we gain our sight."

Develop your own personal navigation system, and release any tendencies or patterns that are actually auto-pilot programs from you past.[5]

You start by getting in touch with four important things:

1. Your values
2. Your vision for your life
3. Your beliefs about life, love, finance, spiritual matters and how the world works
4. Your purposes in the various aspects of your life.

This forms the framework for your next steps in life, for trusting yourself to know who you are, what you think, how you feel and what you want. Without that knowledge, you cannot make decisions that reflect the results you want. You make decisions based on what others told you that you *should* want. Remember, don't let people *should* on you!

When you have a good understanding of those four things above—your values, vision, beliefs and purposes, you can then consider them in light of your relationship with your partner. If most values are shared, life will be easier. If you both have a similar vision for the life you want to share, life will be easier. If your beliefs coincide, or are sufficiently in

---

[5] Bregnan, Peter. "How to Teach Yourself to Trust Yourself." *Harvard Business Review.* http://blogs.hbr.org/2010/11/how-to-teach-yourself-to-trust

sync, life will be easier. If you can support each other's purposes, life will be easier. It's that simple.

Respect

Yes, Aretha Franklin had it right:

> "R-E-S-P-E-C-T
> Find out what it means to me
> R-E-S-P-E-C-T"

Do you know what respect is for you, what it means to you? Do you know what it feels like to have respect for yourself? Dictionary.com defines it this way:

> "to hold in esteem or honor:
> to show regard or consideration for;
> to refrain from intruding upon or interfering with."

So, with that understanding, do you do those things for yourself?

This is BIG. It goes hand-in-glove with honesty, safety and trust.

When G. Charles Andersen and I wrote, *Soul Solitude: Taking Time for Your Soul to Catch Up,*[6] we wrote about an important new element. We call it "You Matter." Most of us need a large dose of "You Matter!"

No one can really give you "You Matter" although some folks are lucky enough to get a sprinkling in their upbringing. It's something you have to grow within yourself. And, when you do, you will respect yourself.

---

[6] Shaler, Rhoberta and Andersen, G. Charles. *Soul Solitude: Taking Time for our Souls to Catch Up.* Humana Press. 2007.

So, Aretha had it right, and The Staple Swingers added to it with their song, *Respect Yourself:*

> "Respect yourself, respect yourself
> If you don't respect yourself
>
> Ain't nobody gonna give a good cahoot,
> Respect yourself, respect yourself."[7]

That's how goes. If you do not respect yourself, it's highly likely that others will not, either. That may help you to understand why it is SO important to do your own work, to work on yourself. First, because you're worth it. Second, because you want to create a life and relationships based on mutual honesty, safety, trust, respect and reliability. And, you know, you cannot give a gift you do not have!

How do you build up respect for yourself? It's definitely an inside job. Here are some insights that can help you:

1. What do you really value? What makes life worth living? When you know what is most important to you, it makes all decision-making easier. It is your foundation.
2. Give up living from other people's expectations of you, and set your own standards. Take back your life.
3. Know that you are always going to be a work-in-progress. No one is perfect and it's nothing to aim for anyway. When others judge or criticize you, take a look at what they are saying and think about it. Does it have value to you? Is it something that you agree would improve your life? If so, take positive action. If not, disregard it.

---

[7] Ingram, Luther Thomas and Mack Rice. *Respect Yourself.*
http://www.metrolyrics.com/respect-yourself-lyrics-the-staple-singers.html

4. If you have made mistakes in life, forgive yourself. Take positive steps to learn from the mistakes so they are not repeated. Then, let them go. Beating yourself up is not respectful.

5. Embrace yourself, flaws and all. Come to peace with the parts of you that are less than perfect and celebrate the parts of you that you love most about yourself. Change what you can and be OK with what you cannot change right now. That's progress!

6. Decide to see the glasses half full, rather than half empty. See what is possible, rather than impossible. See the good in yourself and others, rather than focusing on faults and weaknesses.

7. Create and honor your own pace in life. Give up envy and measuring yourself by what other people are doing, have done, or expect you to do. This is your life. Don't procrastinate because life will pass you by. Step up and step into it fully. Each day is a new beginning. Embrace it.

8. Believe in the choices and decisions you have made. If they need changing, do it. Spend as little time in regret as possible. You cannot change the past, only the present which influences your future. If your decisions are based on your consciously held values, you'll make better and better ones.

9. Ignore the words of others who try to tell you who you are or who you *should* be. Especially ignore those who try to make you feel small, wrong, and inadequate. Those are their issues, not yours. You decide who you are, not them. And, learn to let the haters hate. They do not respect themselves any more than they respect you, or they would not set themselves up as judge and jury.

10. Demonstrate that you have strong convictions. Live from your values and convictions and you'll find that "negative natterers" won't make you question yourself.

11. Respect Others. Treat people the way you want to be treated and you will be able to respect yourself more. It doesn't matter who they are or what they have done. You do it because of who you are, not who they are.

12. Be kind, honest and careful with yourself. Don't harm yourself, insult yourself, steal from yourself, or be dishonest to yourself. People often do and say things to themselves that they would never do or say to someone they really cared about.

13. Teach others how to treat you. People are often thoughtless. They say and do things that make it evident that they have little respect for themselves. How can they respect you? Teach them how to treat you. Tell them what is OK with you AND what is not OK. Do it in ways that are both kind and honest at the same time. Remember, there is never a need for "brutal honesty."

14. Recognize the signs of manipulative and/or controlling relationships. These are unhealthy whether you are doing it or someone is doing it to you. Get help to replace these unhealthy patterns with loving, respectful, effective ones.

15. Recognize that you can give yourself what you need. There is no need to be needy. That is disrespectful in both directions: you do not respect yourself enough to believe you have what it takes, and you do not respect the other person because you want them to take care of you. Stop!

16. Take very good care of yourself, physically, mentally, emotionally and spiritually. No one else can do that for you.

Care enough about yourself to treat yourself well.
That's respect!

Reliability

Reliability is different from trust although it is definitely related. Some people may think this is a distinction without a difference. It may be, but I think it is more important than that and worth sharing with you here.

The difference between *trust* and *reliability* is this:

> RELIABLE: You willingly complete your "honey-do list" when you say you will. You take the responsibility for putting the garbage at the curb, and the house never gets smelly. Ensuring that the car gets its regular maintenance is important to you, so you look after it when it needs to be done. That makes you reliable.

> TRUSTWORTHY: You are excellent at keeping the confidence of your friends. You do not gossip or tell secrets. This makes you trustworthy.

You clearly see the difference now. There are people you can rely on to behave in certain ways but cannot trust with your hearts or lives. And, conversely, there are people you might trust with your life, secrets and money but can't rely on to show up on time for meetings.

Trust has to do with character; reliability has to do with circumstances.

> "Character cannot be developed in ease and quiet. Only through experience of trial and suffering can the soul be strengthened, ambition inspired and success achieved."
> ~ Helen Keller

When you have consciously developed your character, when you have developed the mental and moral qualities that make you who you are, you are ready for prime time. When you add reliability into the mix, you become a star!

Honesty, safety, trust, respect and reliability are the Relational Gifts. You have to have them to give them, or you will move into resentment, build a condo, and live there. You will make others wrong for not having them and not giving them to you, yet you will withhold them from yourself and others. You can easily see that this can erode the relationship with your partner, slowly like water torture, or quickly like torrential rain on a mud cliff. It will wear it away.

Give the Relational Gifts to yourself. If you need help to develop them, get it and get it now. Your life and relationship are in need of them, so don't wait. Work with an experienced counselor to uncover and discover the thoughts, beliefs and events that are obstacles to the process and work them through. Then, you will have the gifts to give to yourself, to your partner and to other people you value.

CHAPTER 6

Your Personal Weather Report

You are likely really good about taking note of the weather each day. It's a general topic of conversation when there is nothing else to say. When dialogue stalls, weather—though obvious to everyone—is the go-to filler.

When you meet someone, it is conventional to use some version of "How are you?" and then your job is done. All too often you don't even stop to hear the answer, OR, really want to know. Yet, you ask.

Most folks are well aware of the convention of asking and give little attention to, or have little intention to, answer it honestly. A simple, on-the-fly *"Fine"* or *"Well"* or *"OK"* seems to suffice, no matter how fabulous or lousy your day actually is. Interesting!

With people you are closer to, you are more likely to ask the question seeking actual information. You *do* want to know how they are. It becomes both the arrival platform of coming together and the departure platform for further, and likely deeper, conversation.

Asking someone how they are with a genuine desire to know the answer sounds different from a casual "How're you doin?'" or "Whassup?" You are looking at each other, making eye contact, and are conveying that you care when you ask "What's new with you?", "How are you feeling?" or "How are things?" You're asking them to give you a weather report from within. The depth of their answer tells you something about the depth of your relationship. Are they safe to give you an accurate answer? Do they trust you with the information? Even more, do they trust that you really care enough for them to tell you the truth?

So, you ask others how they are. Big questions:

How often do you ask yourself how you are?

How often do you give yourself an in-depth answer?

How well do you know what is really going on within you?

It is essential for you to get in touch with what is really going on with your internal "weather system." If you do not know what's going on with you at any time, how can you honestly answer the 'How are you?" question? How can you let someone into your world? How could you ever have an emotionally intimate relationship?

Love, trust and intimacy actually start with you knowing yourself better than you ever have. It's a continuous process, always evolving, ever changing. You must be loving, trusting, and emotionally intimate with yourself. This takes conscious effort. That's why KAIZEN FOR COUPLES is a part of a larger relationship system called Conscious Kaizen™. In order to contribute yourself most honestly and openly to the relationship, you must know yourself. And, likely, you must know yourself better than you do right at this moment.

Most people do not accord themselves the time to stop and listen to what is going on within themselves. I invite you to not be one of them.

You matter. And, first and foremost, you must matter to yourself!

Your Personal Weather Report

Getting in touch with what is really going on inside yourself is a gift you give yourself. You cannot be emotionally intimate with another person without being emotionally intimate with yourself. Susan Campbell, author of *The Couples Journey,*[8] said that she sees the word "intimacy" as four little words: In To Me See. That's helpful to remember.

First, you have to have quiet times alone when you practice "in to me see." Without this, you have nothing to tell or share. Without this, you offer quick, surface, fill-in-the-blanks answers. Without this practice, you may also be asking why you never get your needs met in your relationships. See how key it is!

We live in a world that encourages us to do more, have more, want more. It's no wonder we call ourselves "The Human Race!" The mantra seems to be:

> *"Rush, push, press, stress.*
> *Be more. Do more. Have More.*
> *Repeat!"*

Does that sound at all familiar? Have you recently watched a TV commercial or seen a magazine or newspaper ad that tells you that you can have it all, do it all, and be it all? Those subliminal messages are all around us every day. You walk past the magazine stand and covers scream at you: "Live bigger. Have more." You go online and it gets even

---

[8] Campbell, Susan M. *The Couple's Journey: Intimacy as a Path To Wholeness.* Impact Publishing, 1980.

more persistent and intense: *"How to Make Millions in Fifteen Minutes a Day on the Beach in Bali."* The messages: this is what you *should* want!

- Are you here to have the life someone else tells you that you *should* have or want?
- Are you here to live up to the expectations of others?
- Is it possible that you measure yourself by someone else's expectations of you?
- Have you adopted the "rush, push, press, stress" the world screams at you from every computer screen, magazine, TV and stage?

What if that's the wrong track? Are you willing to look at that? If so, read *Soul Solitude: Taking Time for Our Souls To Catch Up,* and get some insights for thinking through living up to the expectations of others.

For today, you can simply look at what's going on within you at this minute. Get good at your Personal Weather Report, your PWR. Here's how:

Begin by setting aside ninety seconds—ONLY 90 SECONDS!—six to eight times a day to practice. In the beginning, I suggest you set daily alarms on your cell phone to get you in the habit. It is a simple practice of giving yourself an accurate, denial-free weather report of what is going on internally for you at that very moment. You're safe. No one else is listening. You take the time to let you catch up with yourself, as we talk about in *Soul Solitude.* You get in touch with yourself. You create a better relationship with yourself.

Breathing to relax and focus. Purposely structuring how you breathe to accomplish different goals has become much more mainstream now that its yogic roots are better understood and adopted. This breathing pattern for the PWR not only relaxes you but brings you back to yourself. You give this time and attention to yourself to connect with yourself once again. You do a lot of connecting with others in a day, but, if you are like most people, your time for connecting with yourself is almost non-existent. This is conscious connection. It's not giving your attention to something or someone external, like the boss, the news or the TV. It's a gift you give yourself…six to eight times a day.

The Personal Weather Report, your PWR, begins with helping your body relax and revitalize. You do that with your breath, but a special, easy kind of breathing. It's simple, quick, and can be done wherever you are. It's most effective if you can sit while doing it so that your body is supported and your spine is mostly straight.

How To Do The PWR Breathing:

1. Relax in your seat, keeping your back upright and relatively straight, but not posed or rigid. It's fine to lean against the back of the chair.
2. Take a really big breath in through your nose and blow it forcefully out of your mouth.
3. Place your tongue against that soft tissue back of your upper front teeth. Let your tongue sit there easily, with no strain. Keep your tongue there throughout the exercise. That may seem funny when you exhale but you'll get the hang of it.
4. Close your mouth and inhale normally through your nose for a mental count of four.
5. Hold your breath for a count of seven.
6. Exhale completely through your mouth to a count of eight. You will hear the breath leave your body, an audible sound.

That's a ratio of 4:7:8, so this is often just called by its numeric name. It is also known as Relaxing Breath. I first learned it more than thirty years ago while studying pranayama, or yogic breathing. Recently, Dr. Andrew Weil has become a very visible proponent of this very old practice.

It's not about how long each count is. If you find it impossible to exhale that long, speed up the count a bit so that you can manage 4:7:8 breathing in a relaxed way. It's all about increasing your relaxation, not about adding stress by running out of breath! With practice, you will be able to slow down the count and get even more oxygen circulating in your blood stream, and carbon dioxide leaving it.

The Personal Weather Report system begins with breathing to turn your attention quickly to yourself, as well as to relax the body and bring you into the present moment. You can use this breathing any time you want to relax as well. Four full 4:7:8 breaths are usually all you need. If, after a month of practice, you want to extend it to eight breaths because you love the tranquility and focus it brings, go right ahead. You cannot do this too many times a day. But, stick to four breaths at a time until you really feel ready for more. It will take away internal tension. It's a great practice to use when you are feeling anxious, upset, irritated, or unable to sleep. Use it before a meeting, or conversation that you expect to be difficult or charged. Use it before a presentation. I recommend it to all my anger management students, because it works! Oh, and it's a great practice to share with your children, to empower them to take charge when they feel upset, too.

So, that's the preparation for the PWR. If you've tried it as you read the instructions, you'll likely already notice that you feel better. You are more relaxed and you are able to think more clearly.

The next PWR step is to get in touch with what is actually going on in your head, heart and body. Now, keep in mind, this is all going to happen in about ninety seconds, and it takes longer than that to read the instructions!

The Personal Weather Report is simple. It's just not always easy. You are looking within yourself for the most honest answers to these four questions:

1. What am I thinking right now?
2. What am I feeling right now?
3. What do I need right now?
4. What do I want right now?

Sounds simple, right?

It's just not all that easy when you first begin. You are not likely used to getting in touch with what is really going on within you, even when you think you are.

Other people may have taught you to stuff your feelings away. Unlearn that!

Most people have a habit of tucking away their real feelings or judging themselves harshly when an honest feeling arises. They have been taught by others that honest, open, raw, accurate, hard-to-face feelings are somehow unacceptable. You've likely had the experience of feeling close enough to someone in a conversation to share a true feeling or fear. You made yourself vulnerable (and that's a bit scary). Then, the other person had no capacity to be empathetic and s/he said: "You shouldn't feel like that because _____."

Is that familiar? That just shoots you down. Your feelings scare them so they try to make them go away. In doing so, those people also shut out any possibility of deepening both the conversation and the relationship. They don't know what to do with your feelings, and most likely, are not in touch with their own. So, just at the moment you open up, they deflect. When you hear, "You shouldn't feel that way," know that it is very likely that the person you were opening up to is actively closing down. They may be too uncomfortable to look at their own feelings.

When someone tells you, "You shouldn't feel that way," you now know that you have struck a chord in them that they do not want to hear or acknowledge. They are really saying "Please pick a feeling to express that I am comfortable with and willing to discuss."

If you really care about deepening the relationship, one way you can move forward at the moment they *should* on you is to say, "I was sharing my real feeling with you. I wasn't asking for permission to feel that way." Why would you say that? Because most people recoil when they are told "You shouldn't feel that way." They think there is something wrong with them because they actually DO feel that way.

There is nothing wrong with you expressing your real feelings. It is the listener who is giving you more information about them: they cannot go there with you. That's information about him or her, not about you. With that information, you can then choose whether or not you are safe sharing your feelings with that person. You may want to be. . . but you may not be!

This process becomes more difficult when it is your partner that you want to share with, of course. And, it often is the case that your partner cannot, or will not, let conversation go deeper. You'll find answers to that in other places in this book.

Back to the Personal Weather Report. Practice your PWR six to eight times a day.

1. **What am I thinking right now?**
2. **What am I feeling right now?**
3. **What do I need right now?**
4. **What do I want right now?**

Each time it will become a little bit easier. Each time you will be giving yourself permission to explore what is really going on with you. And, you do all this without ever discussing it with anyone. It's **your** practice, just for you. In the next chapter, you'll find out how this becomes a powerful relationship skill that will draw you much closer to your partner, and your partner to you!

A PWR example might be:

> "I think this technique sounds too simple to be effective. I'm annoyed that I have to take on this task when it's really other people who need to change. I want my life to be easier and less stressful, so I want to give this a try so that I have a way to take charge of myself in any situation."

OR

> "I think I'm going to explode if I can't say what I really think to my partner. I feel disrespected and pressured at the same time. I need to figure out a way to talk to him/her and find out what s/he really needs from me. I want to work this out and I know it's not helpful for me to get so angry about this, so, even though I'm scared about doing it, I really want to see if I can talk about this."

That could lead to another PWR based on having just gotten in touch with being scared:

> "Wow! I'm scared. I didn't realize that I really am afraid. That makes sense, I guess, because each time I bring up a problem that I have, s/he thinks I'm blaming and gets angry. I think there must be a way to talk about things that bother each of us. If we cannot seem to do it just by talking together, I think

we need to get some professional help. Yes, I want to find out if s/he agrees."

You see, it's not difficult. It's just very, very honest. It has to be. What could be worse than pretending to yourself that things are not as they really are? That's denial! What could be useful about lying to yourself? Nothing!

In the examples above, you'll see that by allowing yourself to be honest with your thoughts and feelings, you can uncover what it is that you really want and need. Sure, it may be the first baby step and it may not get to the heart of the issue immediately, but you're on your way. Being honest with yourself is absolutely the key. You've already learned about that in the "Do You Have The Gifts to Give?" chapter. If you are not honest with yourself, you cannot be honest with your partner. The PWR is the beginning of that honesty.

Off you go. Right this minute. No procrastinating. Put down the book and practice giving yourself a PWR.

> *If you just caught yourself saying,*
> *"Oh, I get it. I don't need to practice."*
> *Notice that is you putting it off.*
> *You are short-changing yourself.*

Don't worry. That's common. Actually paying attention to yourself as if you really matter is foreign to most people! This is the beginning of changing all that, right this minute.

So, put down the book and do the PWR breathing and give yourself a Personal Weather Report, reflecting exactly what is going on within you right now.

No matter what happens in your relationship with your partner, you're on your way to building a better relationship with yourself.

The good news is that having a better relationship with yourself is the best way to have a better relationship with your partner!

CHAPTER 7

Sharing the Personal Weather Report

You want to be known, heard, seen, appreciated, acknowl-edged and accepted. We all do. It's good. It's ideal. It's healthy. It's wise. Yet, so few people seem to feel that way in their relationship with their significant others. And, there is a good reason for that: in order to be able to know, hear, see, appreciate, acknowledge and accept another person, you have to be able to know, hear, see, appreciate, acknowledge and accept yourself!

Once again, the Personal Weather Report will help you with that. AND, it's something you have to work on within yourself. Of course, you can shortcut that journey by working with an experienced counselor or therapist, but even still, it's a journey you have to take alone. A very worthwhile journey!

There are obvious reasons why it is ideal for you and your partner to under-take KAIZEN FOR COUPLES together: it makes sense that both partners agree on their best next steps. That is what this book offers you.

Of course, if your partner isn't interested or ready at this time, you are making a giant contribution to the health of your relationship by work-ing through all these concepts on your own.

When you and your partner are both familiar with the PWR, and have been practicing it independently for a while, you'll find this chapter a logical next step to strengthening and deepening your relationship. If you're doing this on your own, you will know that you are approaching your partner with more honesty, clarity and willingness. That is just wise.

Using Your Personal Weather Report...when you've had a bad day.

Imagine that you had a really bad day at work: deadlines, dismissiveness, doubts and difficulties. You don't want to bring that home with you so, you take the time to give yourself a PWR to find some honest words about what is really going on within you. Doing this may alleviate some of the anger, powerlessness or irritation you feel by simply giving it a name, and knowing exactly where it came from. It can also prevent you from mindlessly taking out the aggravation of the day on the people you say you love most.

It's always wise to create this kind of "transition time" between major portions of your day and your life. It will definitely help you feel both in touch with and in control of yourself in positive productive ways. This is one way of using the PWR to help your relationship with yourself **and** with your partner, even though your partner is not present!

After doing this, you may have dissipated the energy of the "bad day" enough to now focus on going home to your partner without it. Follow this by imagining where you are going next and how you want to be when you get there. There is real power in doing this. Maya Angelou, Oprah's mentor, said, "The greatest gift you can give to anyone is to light up when they come into the room." It works in reverse very well. If you start imagining your next step—how you will light up when you see your partner—it helps it to happen.

If you take yourself through remembering how much you love, respect and care for your partner before you see him or her, you are much more likely to bring that to your first words and touches when you are to-gether. This is Conscious Kaizen:[9] creating your life and relationships purposefully, thoughtfully, skillfully, consciously. You can easily see that you can change your interactions when you change your perspective and practices. Conscious Kaizen will walk you through.

Using Your Personal Weather Report... when something is bothering you or your partner

You'll remember that three of the Relational Gifts are honesty, safety and trust. When something is bothering you—something outside or inside your relationship—you have to be able to be honest about it. And, it has to be able to be spoken of in a relationship where you are safe and can trust the other person with your thoughts, feelings, wants and needs. In other words, it has to be possible to give your Personal Weather Report and have it land in a receptive place. That receptive place is ideally the relationship you have with your partner.

If you are in a relationship where it is not possible to give a PWR with-out provoking defensiveness, selfishness or dismissal, you likely do not feel safe doing so. You know for sure that you are unsafe and cannot trust your partner if s/he says one of these things often in response to your PWR:

- "You shouldn't feel like that because _____."
- "You think you've got problems. Here's what happened to me."

---

[9] Conscious Kaizen™ is an in-depth program created by Dr. Rhoberta Shaler to help you change your life and relationships from the inside out.
Visit www.OptimizeCenter.com to learn more about upcoming relationars and weekend programs.

- "Well, that's your problem. It has nothing to do with me."
- "You're always complaining about something."
- "When are you going to grow up and solve your own problems?"
- "I think you are wrong."
- "It's always about you."

If any of those responses come from your partner habitually, then it's no wonder you've chosen to read KAIZEN FOR COUPLES.

Of course, if any of those responses come from *you* when listening to a PWR from your partner, hopefully you'll have just had a big wake-up call reading those words, too . . . and are now past denying it!

None of those responses is useful for deepening, strengthening or growing your relationship. It will never allow either of you to feel known, seen, heard, appreciated, acknowledged or accepted by one another.

Take heart! There is a better way.

Responding lovingly to a Personal Weather Report

This is big! There is a best way to respond lovingly to a weather report.

When you or your partner want or need to bring up a topic or an issue that might be difficult to hear or discuss, the PWR is invaluable.

Recently, I was working with a couple who each thought they were really good at assessing situations, particularly in those areas where they were having conflict and confrontation with each other. And, it was true…in their own minds. Each could certainly state, with a good deal of conviction, what they believed would solve the relationship problems.

Their answers: the other person had to change.

You know,

> "If only you would do this differently, we wouldn't have a problem."

So common. When couples come to me for the first time, usually the bubbles over their heads say something similar:

> "If only s/he would change, our relationship would be fine."

That's not true in most cases. It takes two people to have a relationship and, when you are focused on what is wrong with your partner, not only are you not looking at your partner in a balanced way, you are not looking at yourself. That's why the PWR is so important.

Here's an example from a couple who had been separated for a few months but came to me to "be sure we're not making a mistake." They had two children who had been witnessing their fighting and the growing distance between them. That's why they wanted to be sure that separating permanently was the right thing to do. Interesting that they were willing to figure that out for the sake of the children, but not for their own sakes!

It took them several weeks to be able to give honest PWR's to themselves and, therefore, to each other. It's not easy when you first begin. You are simply not used to thinking about what is actually going on with you. It's always easier to look at the other person.

There is a big caveat when moving on from giving yourself a PWR to giving one to your partner: You cannot say the word "you!"

No one likes to be blamed. Do you frequently (ever) tell your partner:

- What s/he is failing to do
- What s/he does too often or too much
- What s/he *should* do
- What is wrong with him or her
- Why what s/he is doing is ruining the relationship
- Why what s/he is doing is dancing on your last nerve
- Why you have one foot out the door

Right? If you examine your words when confronting your partner, it is highly likely that they include some combination of those things . . . and, that's not going to work for you!

When you both know how to use the PWR, you change that kind of confrontation forever. You replace it with insightful, thoughtful sharing that allows you both to feel more honest, safe, trusting, and respectful. That closes the ever-widening gap between you created by the blame and shame of accusation.

Your Personal Weather Report is about you,
and you alone.

You want to feel known, seen, heard, appreciated, acknowledged and accepted and so does your partner. It is basic to being human. In fact, William James, deemed to be the father of modern psychology, said:

"The deepest principle in human nature is the craving to be appreciated."

We humans are amazing at withholding appreciation, yet it is so easy to express. And, it costs us nothing!

Exercise your appreciation muscles: find something genuine to appreciate in people and say so. It is essential that it be genuine because flattery will be easily discerned and dismissed. It changes your viewpoint and refreshes your soul immediately.

> *The Personal Weather Report is as effective for expressing what you appreciate as for expressing what troubles you.*

A PWR is an invaluable skill and tool for expressing what is going on within you, and only you. It is easy—and will become effortless—when practiced enough.

- Begin by focusing on what you appreciate in your partner and express it in your PWR to yourself.
- Practice giving your PWR about what you admire, appreciate, and are grateful for in your partner.
- Do it honestly and genuinely. Anything less than that is perfunctory and can be readily recognized as "buttering up." That removes trust quicker than a hot knife through butter!

When your relationship is rocky, your partner may be suspicious when you begin offering sincere appreciation. You may need to assure your partner that you are sincerely interested in changing the nature of your part in your relationship. If you are not both reading KAIZEN FOR COUPLES—and I recommend each having your own copy to read, highlight and return to—then that assurance is imperative. Making the shift from a negative focus to a positive one is often suspect. Allay your partner's concerns by learning together.

CHAPTER 8

The Relationship Kaizen Convercycle

U se the Relationship Kaizen Convercycle™ to make talking together and creating solutions easier. It will strengthen your relationship and give you the confidence—as well as the roadmap—for making the small, consistent, positive changes that benefit your relationship.

First of all—and most importantly—you need a formula, blueprint, map or guideline to work with to take these small Kaizen steps. It's important that they are small so they are doable. There are four main parts to the Relationship Kaizen System as you will discover. Here we apply them to KAIZEN FOR COUPLES particularly, although you'll soon see how well they can be applied to all relationships with just a little thought.

No matter what task or change you undertake in life, it's always best to break it down into small, doable pieces. You cannot do broad sweeping changes all at once any more than you can do a project all at once. Change your thinking on this to reduce your sense of overwhelm immediately. (If you want more help doing that, read my ebook, *How to Eat an Elephant*, available online.) And, the good news is that you can apply these same concepts to your relationship, too.

Whether you call it a system, formula, blueprint or map, it brings with it powerful information gleaned from many who have already used it to arrive at their chosen destinations.

Each traveler is different, but the road remains the same. The map remains constant, while the territory can be a surprise. Every journey to change is different. And, on any journey, you can be waylaid by surprising detours and tempting parking places. Sometimes those parking places become campgrounds, and you stay for a time, complaining all the while of limited options and inadequate resources. Maybe you need a new map that makes it enticing, encouraging and empowering to move on, to shut down the lean-to, and get going.

The Convercycle is such a map. It will take you over, under, around and through new terrain safely. Of course, there will be hills and valleys, rain forests and deserts. That's the nature of a long journey, and it is also part of the adventure, the newness, the exploration.

Your partner is your chosen traveling companion. Traveling companions often find themselves interested in different activities, and wanting to see different sites than one another. They can see this as a shared adventure in learning and life, or as an annoying, unnecessary and undesirable constant negotiation that ruins the trip. That's all about your perspective and your expectations.

If you want your traveling companion to magically turn into your clone, you are going to have a miserable journey! No question. It's going to be about fighting for your supposed "rights" and trying to manipulate outcomes. It will be a drag, and you'll complain to other wayfarers along the road, trying to engage them in your own pity party.

You'll try to convince those you travel with, or simply meet at an evening campfire, that you are a martyr, a saint, a victim, or a superior being. Your thoughts and feelings may be tying you up and holding you down but, in your mind, it's your partner who is causing your distress, your partner who is making life miserable, and your partner who is keeping you from the life you deserve.

Poppycock! It's you. Whatever heavy rocks you would like to put into your traveling companion's backpack, it is you who is obsessed with making the journey difficult. You may be loading up your partner in an effort to lighten your load, but it isn't working, and it won't work. (Now, of course, two people in a partnership can be doing this same thing!)

Yes, people have faults and flaws. All people, that is. And, of course, that includes you.

- Are you fixated on the faults and flaws of others?
- Are you sure that your life would be much better if only your partner was not such a mess?
- Are you convinced that you are being dragged through rough terrain, and that kicking, screaming and complaining are your only alternatives for being noticed as the victim you are?
- Are you sure that you and your partner have different maps and entirely different guidebooks? And, are you also sure that yours is right?

That's harsh, but important. You may have said no to every item above, and yet you recognize the territory. You may not be experiencing those extremes, but the feeling is familiar.

Just by reading that list, you are likely realizing that you might need a new map, a new way to interact, communicate, and create solutions together. The Convercycle can help you get back on track to the shared destination you both wanted to reach when you committed yourselves to each other.

The Convercycle is so simple, yet it is not necessarily easy. That's because you both have to be willing and committed enough to each other, and to the relationship, to engage with it. That's the mystery of something so simple.

You are likely to say "Right. Got it. That's obvious." And then go on your merry way. You were just given gold and you walked away from it, assuming that the idea, the understanding, immediately became part of your personal operating system. It didn't. Don't do that with this! There is no magic. You have to think, decide, and practice before this will become second nature to you. This simple, straightforward process can change the dynamics of your relationship in the way you have longed for, BUT, only if you give it its due.

> *If you say you want your relationship to grow, prosper and flourish but fail to consciously and frequently set aside time to talk with your partner using The Convercycle, your behavior speaks louder than your words. And, your behavior tells the truth!*

I remember a couple who came to see me because they were dissatisfied, unhappy and on the verge of splitting. They had four children and a flourishing business they had built from nothing. They *said* they wanted to get back to the loving, appreciative, respectful way they had been with each other years before.

After a few sessions of learning more about their journey together, I gave them an assignment: before our meeting the next week, set aside four half-hour periods of undistracted time to talk together. No agenda beyond actually being with each other without children, work or other distractions. No agenda beyond being with each other and interested in each other. Simple attention.

The next week they returned and I was curious to hear what they had learned in their times together. So, I asked how the four points of connection had been for them. Here's their answer:

"Oh, we didn't do that. There was no time."

Really? You want me to believe that in 168 hours there were not four half hours in which to connect? That is a demonstration of complete lack of willingness!

In debriefing it with them, it came clear that he had found time for golf and a few beers with his buddies. She had found time for a day trip to a spa with friends and had chosen to go grocery shopping one night while her partner was home. Hmm.

You might be thinking that those are reasonable uses of time and some variation of "s/he deserves to have fun" and, at another time in their relationship, that could be true. But, these folks *said* they were desperate to restore their relationship to a place of being best friends. They *said* that was the most important thing to them. Yet, their choices and behavior said otherwise!

Of course, I pointed all that out to them and they started in with their excuses. Each excuse vanished in the light of the priorities they had stated. They brought up things like this:

- "I work hard and I need some downtime, some time to play and relax."
- "No one should be deprived of a little fun in life."
- "I had already planned the outing with my friends, so I just had to go."

- "The kids take up a lot of our time and we're tired when they go to bed."
- "I can't just stop working, you know!"
- "I was too busy to put something new in the schedule."

OK. Plausible excuses someone might buy, but not me. When you *say* that you really want your relationship to work and you are given a simple assignment that will definitely help and you don't do it, it is simple logic that tells you that you really don't want what you say you most want.

So, what was really going on? After much talking and many tears, they got to it when one said:

> "I think I'm actually afraid to just BE with my partner. Being busy is safer."

That was a breakthrough for both of them. It opened the door to a wonderful conversation about how they had learned to put things between them.

- Kids were very convenient.
- Long hours at work allowed for "reasonable" avoidance.
- Household tasks must be done.
- We have different interests.
- Volunteer jobs made for justifiable absences.
- Parents could not be ignored.
- The business requires our attention.
- Church is a priority.

When they saw those things written down on the white board, they began to realize that they had a litany of justifiable ways of avoiding one another. Not that all those things are not true to some degree, but that they made them ironclad to avoid any possible potential pain.

The trouble with that is that they were both already in great pain. Avoidance clearly had not helped them! Each felt alone, resentful, lonely, upset, angry and afraid, yet neither was willing to take the step offered to them that would lead them out of the fear pit that their relationship had become.

I'm happy to tell you that we went slowly together to work through their issues and to create new attitudes, skills and patterns that allowed them to restore their relationship and make it even better than ever before. They turned their resistance and fear into willingness. That's a big step. They did it using KAIZEN FOR COUPLES strategies and insights. And, you can, too!

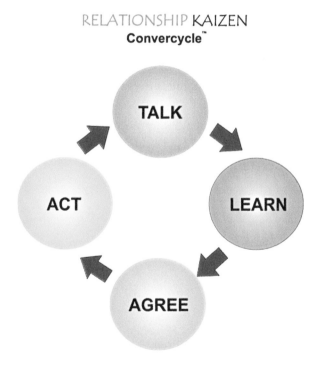

RELATIONSHIP KAIZEN
Convercycle™

The Convercycle is key to transforming your relationship. It does take a commitment to talking together on the very day either of you discovers a pain point, a need or a want. There is never a *good* time for a difficult conversation.

Putting off hard conversations is just accumulating pain and resentment while building fear and anxiety, and postponing possibilities for a solution.

Just reading that sentence may be enough for you to say "No more!"

Yes, you may resonate with the experience of those clients of mine, and keep yourself so busy that there is no time to connect.

Yes, you may be fearful and anxious about tough conversations.

Yes, you may have a history together of failed communications and in-effective conflict management, but it doesn't have to stay that way.

Using The Convercycle is a gentle way to take one teeny, tiny area of discomfort in your relationship and work with it to find a sustainable solution. Just one! Teeny-tiny!

How to Make the The Convercycle Work for You

It may look simple. But where do you start?

That's the beauty of the Convercycle: there are several possible entry points.

TALK leads to LEARN when you listen.
If you ACT it will hopefully lead to TALK.
If you AGREE and ACT, it, too, will lead to TALK.

The natural progression, though, when using it very consciously, is to start at TALK. Remember that Kaizen—small, incremental, conscious improvements—means that it is important to **TALK about small issues, too. If you have a big issue or two, you begin by breaking the big issue down to one small thing that you think would really help. Practice it. Notice the results. TALK again.**

One of the major problems with couples and their problem-solving habits is that they want to fix the big issues first. That is overwhelming. It leads to frustration and resentment, and all too often, to relationship breakdown. Here's an example of how to break down a big issue:

> Recently I was working with a couple who have been married eighteen years. Almost from the beginning, issues showed up, big issues. In fact, after a couple of sessions, it became clear that the husband has very deep passive-aggressive traits, and after eighteen years of living together, the wife had learned to fight fire with fire: she began to behave in passive-aggressive ways to "show him what it feels like!"

Unfortunately, that is not uncommon. It takes two people for one person to be passive-aggressive. But, in her attempt to have him experience the frustration of living with him, the relationship was teetering on the brink of breakup.

I wrote an ebook, *Stop! That's Crazy-Making*, and created a free checklist at PassiveAggressiveChecklist.com. I am very familiar with the signs, symptoms, behaviors and underlying struggles that produce passive-aggressive behavior.

> This couple found me online while in a frantic last-ditch effort to find help. They came to me in the last gasps of a close-to-dying relationship.

These two had been experiencing a very common passive-aggressive pattern in terms of the The Convercycle: extensive TALK, intention to LEARN but too fearful, hurt and resentful to listen well, and AGREE. Where they got repeatedly stuck was that, after AGREE, ACT did not seem to look remotely like what AGREE had worked out. This is the passive-aggressive pattern.

For this couple to continue on The Convercycle constructively, they had to break down the passive-aggressive pattern into small topics. It was so tempting for the wife to simply say:

"There you go again, being your passive-aggressive self. Why do I put up with this?"

That gets them nowhere good. Both are aware of the pattern, and neither is doing anything about it. They think they are, but they are not. And, labeling does not help!

They think there is a "win" in identifying the over-arching pattern. She wants him to witness her frustration. She thinks they are communicating and, therefore, helping the situation resolve.

For him, it is another blow, another repetition of the label he has now grown to hate. Neither partner is doing anything to rectify or improve the situation, really. Being able to name a pattern is a good start, but then you have to claim it and tame it. With these two, they have the naming, but the claiming and the taming? Not so much.

The Convercycle opens the door for change, but only when you practice breaking the issue into small enough parts.

KAIZEN FOR COUPLES invites you to choose one small thing, learn as much as you can from each other about it, agree on the best next step, and then take action.

For this couple, one of those small parts was isolated:

> She: "I feel so let down and confused when promises don't seem to mean anything. I want and need to be able to rely on promises. When I get your agreement that you will do something by a certain time, that's a promise in my books. You tell me you will do something for me or the family, and you promise. When I ask you if you have done it, you tell me that you did not have time. That is one thing that drives me up the wall."

> He: "Well, I didn't have time."

> She: "That's not the issue, really. The issue is promising and then not fulfilling the promise. Part of making the promise is knowing there is time to fulfill it, don't you think?"

> He: "I don't want you to be upset if I tell you that I cannot do what you want, so I just promise. I guess some part of me doesn't want the conflict in the moment, so I promise."

> She: "I would be so much happier with hearing that you honestly may not be able to do it, rather than be disappointed when it isn't done and I was counting on it."

> He: "You would be OK with that?"

> She: "I would certainly be OK with that. I might not be happy about it because we would have to work something out to get things done. What is important to me is being able to talk

honestly and solve problems together. When promises are broken, that feels much worse to me than hearing that it might not be possible in the first place."

He: "You really wouldn't think I'm a loser if I just tell you I don't think I can get it done?"

She: "No, it would feel like honest partnership, and that is what I want. I would be much happier working out how to get something done together, than thinking that it is handled and then being disappointed, upset, or let down."

He: "I feel like a loser when I know I can't do something you want done. And, now that we're talking about it, I guess I get angry when you ask me to do things all the time. Maybe that's part of why I don't do them."

She: "Angry?"

He: "Yes, I resent it. I have so little time when I'm not working and the list of things you want done seems to grow all the time. Yeah, I resent it."

She: "I work, too, so I know what that feels like. Are you saying that I ask too much of you?"

He: "I guess so. And, it makes me mad and that makes me dig my heels in and just let things slide. Yeah, that's how I really feel!"

She: "How long have you felt that way?"

He: "For years, now that I think about it."

She: "So, that's why you don't do what you promised so frequently?"

He: "Yep."

She: "Maybe I'm not very open when you tell me you cannot do something I want you to do because I feel I have so much on my plate to do."

He: "And, I feel I have so much on my plate and you always want to add more."

She: "Could we make an agreement then? I'll work at being more open to the possibility that you cannot do what I am asking."

He: "I'll work on telling you right when you ask whether or not I really think I can do what you're asking. That's going to be tough for me because I'll still be afraid that you'll be unhappy about it."

She: "I may be unhappy about it, but I'll do my best to listen to you and accept what you are saying, because it would make me much happier in the long run."

He: "OK. Let's try that."

She: "Agreed."

This may or may not work the first time or two, but the point is to return to TALK and listen to each other to find out what's really going on, LEARN. Then see where the points of agreement are and what you can now AGREE to again. And, around it goes to ACT…and back to TALK and….

For many couples not dealing with well-entrenched passive-aggressive traits, this is also the place where things stall. *That is why it is a cycle.* As soon as ACT is not in alignment with AGREE, TALK has to happen. That is why it is so important to be committed to the process.

The good news is that couple is slowly changing their patterns with each other. That's not the biggest payoff, though. They are actively talking with each other about things that really matter to each of them. They are learning that, with small steps, things can change. Even when they are agreeing on what doesn't work, they are still agreeing, and behaviors are slowly changing and a more harmonious pattern is developing.

Their communication didn't get into difficulty quickly . . . it took years to develop that pattern. They recognize that it will take a while to get back into harmony. But, they are still committed to the process, and that's the most important thing!

There are going to be bumps, hiccups, falls and stumbles. No one is perfect. A good idea is to think of all the variables that comprise your relationship as cats. Your commitment to each other is to generally herd the cats west! As long as each of you keeps your focus on arriving at a loving, honest, safe, respectful, trusting, reliable relationship, you will benefit…and the cats will arrive safely, too.

CHAPTER 9

The Six RelationSteps

I t sounds so simple: six steps to save, sustain and strengthen your relationship. And, it is. It's just not quick and not always easy! After all, if it were easy, you would have done it by yourselves years or months ago, right?

This is not one of those books that you can read just a half a chapter and think you know what to do. This is a whole system, and a system works best taken as a whole...if you want the very best results it can provide for you.

These six RelationSteps will take you in the right direction. If they were a map, they would get you to the right country, state, province and city. You need the other chapters to find your exact address, to get to the place you want to call home. That's the place where you are safe: you are seen, heard, known, appreciated, acknowledged and accepted. It's a great place! Let's go.

You've likely noticed that you don't live in a vacuum. There are people all around. Some are having a great day, others not so much. Some want to lift you up and others want to drag you down. Some are aware. Others are running on auto-pilot. And, you may well be just like them on different days of the week—and so is your partner.

One of the most common complaints I hear in my private practice is "S/he is not the person I married."

Think about it: would you really want to be in relationship with that younger version of your partner now? Sure, you remember things fondly because of the rose-colored glasses of infatuation and the excitement at finding one another. But, life has intervened. Hopefully, *neither* of you are the same as you were then. And, hopefully, you have both changed and grown into more aware, accepting, alive, mature human beings. Yet, some folks hold onto the fantasy that everything would be perfect if his or her partner was "like they were when we got married."

Another problem with believing in that whole fantasy is that likely, in the back of your mind, when you got married, you actually thought there was room for improvement in your new spouse and you were just the person to change him or her! You were going to mold, redesign, take off the rough edges, and smooth him or her into the perfect partner. How's that working for you?

It's a double-edged sword. You want the fantasy of the infatuation but with the changes you envisioned all in place and ready to respond to you with appreciation, love and even passion for being the Svengali— the magician, the change-artist—you were willing to be. Darn! It doesn't work that way.

You've likely noticed that people resist being told what to do and how to be. You don't like it and neither do they. You want to change him/her and s/he wants you to stay just the same as the day s/he fell in love with you. Or, vice versa. This is an issue that needs wrestling to the ground.

*REALITY CHECK:
it's not your job to change anybody!*

Trying to change someone else often stems from an unwillingness to look at yourself. It's so much easier to find fault and give supposedly constructive advice to someone else, rather than look in the mirror and do your own work.

And, you can only do *your own work*. You cannot do someone else's. So you've focused on an impossible task if you think you will change your partner.

OK, before you go too far down the rabbit hole with your head swimming, let's talk about what you CAN do that can make life together more peaceful, more insightful, more loving, more supportive and more intimate. It's always best to focus on what you *can* do. That's the entire point of Kaizen: small—sometimes tiny—doable positive changes that lead you to what is possible for you as a couple.

Often, couples come to my office, as I've said, and want *the* big problem **fixed**! They want the pain to go away. Unrealistically, they want the pain to go away in the next hour, with little or no work. I have to remind them that they didn't get to this troubling place quickly and the road to a much more peaceful place is also going to be long, and occasionally rocky.

The good news is that the map exists and you are holding it in your hand. So, no overnight solutions, salvages or saving, but a steady walk on a tried and true path will get you where you most want to go.

NOTE: You may think you know where you want to go. You may both be willing to go there. Yet, sometimes, after travelling this new road together, couples find that their destination was either unavailable, or was a journey for one alone.

This happens. Celebrate!

If you find that you learn to talk well together, solve problems and make agreements, you'll be able to share the decision to walk on separately. It's not the end of the world. You've learned things about yourself, your values, your vision, beliefs and purposes, and you take all that with you. You will separate in far more loving, peaceful ways once you have uncovered and discovered what you both most want. That's a different kind of mutuality. **And, it is not a failure.**

Here is your map. As you would with any map, you have to orient yourself correctly. You have to know where you are. Although you can begin anywhere, the best place to start is Self-Awareness.

KAIZEN RELATIONSTEPS™

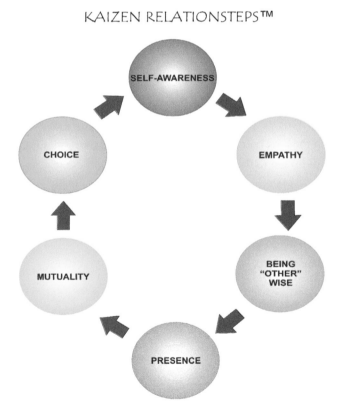

Self-Awareness

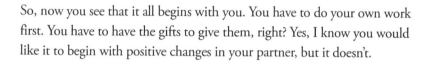

- Who are you?
- What do you value?
- How do you demonstrate what you value?
- What is your vision for your life, where you are going and how you are going to get there?
- What are your beliefs about life, love, others, the world and spiritual matters?
- What is your purpose in each arena of your life?

So, now you see that it all begins with you. You have to do your own work first. You have to have the gifts to give them, right? Yes, I know you would like it to begin with positive changes in your partner, but it doesn't.

It begins with you.

It is only when your words, thoughts and actions are in alignment with your values, vision, beliefs and purpose that you can live in integrity and find inner calmness. It is only then that you begin to see others clearly. You have to get your own ducks in a row first. Until then, you are hoping to make people do and be what and how you want them to be, focusing outside yourself while failing to do your own work.

That's what starts arguments.

"Why can't you just do it my way?"

"Why can't you be more like me?"

Do you see that? Is it possible that that is your main idea of what needs to happen in your relationship? If so, you now have a new insight: Focus on yourself for a while. You need to become self-aware, to see yourself as you really are and work towards being the person you want to be.

When people come to my anger management classes, I am encouraged that they will benefit from the learning when they start by saying this:

"I don't like who I am when I get angry."

That's the key piece for progress. If you see yourself clearly in an area of your life, and you don't like what you are seeing, that is the beginning of self-awareness AND the beginning of positive change.

Self-awareness is having a good look at where you currently are in your thinking, feeling, wants and needs. It is being able to use the Personal Weather Report frequently and effectively to get in touch with what is really going on within you. That's the starting place for the journey to self-awareness.

Then ask yourself: Am I hurting anyone with my words, actions or choices? That anyone includes hurting yourself.

Self-awareness requires that you step out of any fog, any denial, and look at yourself and what you are doing. So often people put themselves at the bottom of their list of people they care about. They make promises to themselves that they fail to keep. They treat themselves shabbily, usually in their heads where no one knows . . . they think. But, it shows. It shows in the ways they think about, address and treat others. It cannot help but show.

Becoming aware of the possibly shabby way you relegate yourself to the bottom of your list in the ways you care for and respect yourself is an eye-opener. Who ever said you don't deserve better treatment? Who taught you that? How do you unlearn it? Knowing where the lessons came from helps you to get a more objective view of yourself.

My mother was a fearful, angry, hurt woman. If you asked her, she would tell you that was absolutely wrong. Of course, that was her style: everyone else was wrong and she was right. In her mind she was strong, right and righteous, and she believed her own press. It was hard, if not impossible, for her to notice and comment on the good she saw in her world and the people in it. She simply withheld her approval, and generously donated her negative assessments. She was a well-seasoned fault-finder and not afraid to share her views. You might know someone like her. Or, maybe you see her in your own mirror on your worst days.

Being raised by someone like that caused me to do a lot of fancy dancing and second-guessing. Dancing to get her approval, and second-guessing my own sanity. The way she saw things and the way I saw things were miles—as well as generations—apart!

My mother took a strong stand with a strong voice for what she believed to be true. My mother was a racist. Enough said. You can see how that is hurtful. Even as a child, it was hurtful to me because I could not understand why the color of a person's skin or the language they spoke, or the clothes they wore was cause for such ire, rage and outrage. She had much to say about it at home where she was happy to have her opinions, edicts and pronouncements taken as gospel truth. It didn't fly with me, but it did create a "How to Keep The Giants Happy" predicament.

My mom was not self-aware. She knew what she didn't like or want, that's true. However, she failed to see that her words, actions and choices might be causing many people to avoid her, if not outright detest or dismiss her.

Yes, it's true that she had the absolute right to her opinions and the right to express them in ways she felt were appropriate. Knowing what you think, feel and believe is definitely part of self-awareness. That is not in question. While she needed to feel justified and righteous to quell her own insecurities, her behavior made others fearful of her. It caused her further fear, hurt, frustration, anger...and justification. Her behavior isolated her from many aspects of her society, and of course, to her it was all their fault.

That's an extreme example, but it might have some meaning for you. Here are other extreme views that you might find just a little truth in when you're truly honest with yourself:

- Are you aware of your impact on people?
- Are you vocal in your opinions and maybe try to force them on others?
- Do you think you are the only one with the right answer, view or solution?
- Do you treat others as though they have a lot to learn and you have it to teach them?
- Do you expect others to ask "How high?" when you say jump?
- Is there any "my way or the highway" in your attitude?
- Do you spend time, focus and energy on blaming, shaming, judging and justifying?

Do you know where you came by your approach to life and other people? Have you examined it to see how it is impacting your health, happiness and relationships recently?

You might think "Oh, that's just the way I am." Remember, you are choosing the way you are at every moment. No one is forcing you. You are choosing it. There is no one to blame, as much as you wish there were, or think there was. That's what happens when you become an emotional grown-up!

Maybe you missed the memo!
Emotional grown-ups accept that there is no one to blame
for their current thoughts, words, attitudes and actions.
They accept full responsibility for them and their
consequences.

The journey to self-awareness is an inside job. No one can do it for you although you can certainly benefit from working with a counselor to uncover, discover and recover what can make a huge difference in your level of self-awareness. When you work with someone, it keeps you focused on the process and consistently moving forward. When you don't, life intervenes and you get put back at the bottom of your list. Is that what you want?

Empathy

Empathy requires engagement with another person. It is active, not passive. It is the essence of the old phrase, "walking a mile in another person's moccasins." It is different from sympathy.

Empathy: the power of understanding and imaginatively entering into another person's feelings.[10]

Sympathy: the fact or power of sharing the feelings of another, especially in sorrow or trouble; compassion or commiseration.[11]

---

[10] *Collins English Dictionary - Complete & Unabridged 10th Edition* 2009 © William Collins Sons & Co. Ltd. 1979, 1986 © HarperCollins
[11] Dictionary.com Unabridged. Based on the Random House Dictionary, © Random House, Inc. 2014.

They are both feelings concerning other people. You can think of it as sympathy is "feeling with" another, and empathy is "feeling into" another, imagining yourself in their circumstances. If you've been in their shoes, you feel empathy. If you haven't, you feel sympathy.

Empathy keeps you connected with the other but sufficiently separate to be helpful.

Sympathy can be appropriately supportive but not actively helpful.

Empathy is a deeper emotional experience because you are putting yourself in the other's shoes for a little while. Empathy allows you to share an unspoken understanding. You are fully there with the other person, acknowledging their pain, joy or growth because you know how it feels when you experience it. Sympathy means you think you know what another is going through. It is a more collective term. You can offer sympathy at a funeral, for example, but, unless you have actually lost a loved one, you cannot empathize in a deeply self-referential way.

Why are these distinctions important? Because to fully engage with a person you love, you have to be able to empathize with them. You have to open yourself to feeling what they are, may be, or think they are feeling, and let them know that you relate to what they are experiencing.

You don't jump in their boat with them. No, not in the way that you both get lost! That would not help. You jump in with them in order to let them know that you are really understanding what they are going through. You have to hold the lifeline and not get lost in the feeling, too.

Both sympathy and empathy involve caring, but sympathy is more in the sense of compassion for someone in a less fortunate situation than you presently are. You may have sympathy for those starving or tortured in the world. Empathy is generally more personal, shared with someone you know and care about.

It is possible to be empathetic without being sympathetic at the same time and you may need to practice this in your relationship with your partner. A good example would be that you may feel empathy for the distraught sense of loss your partner has when s/he loses all his or her money gambling. You may even try to help him/her analyze the reason s/he lost it all. You are unlikely to be sympathetic, though, because s/he chose to do it and it is his or her fault for taking the chance of losing.

Conversely, you may be both empathetic and sympathetic at the same time. When someone you know loses someone special to cancer, for instance, you are sympathetic for their loss. If you have ever lost a loved one to cancer, you will also be empathetic because you actually know what it feels like to go through such a thing.

Empathy is an important communication skill for your relationship. If you cannot empathize with the person who you say is most important to you, you will not develop emotional intimacy. It is not possible.

Being "Other" Wise

Just as being able to put yourself briefly in another person's shoes leads to greater emotional intimacy, so does the willingness and skills you bring to the relationship. Empathy is essential to building intimacy. Insights, skills, fears, hurts and prior challenging situations and successes are all part of the package each of you brings into the relationship.

Often, in the early throes of romance, you don't think about where your new "love" has come from, what s/he has been through, or, what baggage may have been claimed. You were more focused on seeing the best in him or her, excusing and overlooking the parts you didn't like so much, and pursuing the dream of being loved and loving. The rose-colored glasses were working overtime.

You're not alone. Most people do exactly the same thing. You want to be known, seen, heard, appreciated, acknowledged and accepted. You want that special someone whose heart beats just for you. That's human. That's the longing everyone has in their heart of hearts. So, no blame, no shame for wanting it, too.

You looked at your potential mate with those famous rose-colored glasses and failed to see the humanness, the flaws, the faults, the red flags. And s/he looked at you in just the same way. That's what biology sets you up for. That's why it is called the biological imperative: the need of living organisms to perpetuate their existence. And, biology is powerful and likes to win!

I had a young couple who came for counseling . . . very shortly after their wedding. Both were angry and close to tears when they walked in. They were frustrated, disappointed, and scared. Each said:

> "I didn't think marriage would be like this. I thought that 'happily ever after' just came from making those promises to each other."

Naïve? Yes, of course. They were young and inexperienced. They honestly believed that marriage would transform their petty differences into loving quirks. They thought that a ceremony would make them different. They thought that love was enough.

Love isn't enough. You may think that is harsh but it is true. Love simply isn't enough.

Love can be "a horrible master and a terrible monster" (Kinder, 2011)[12] when you think that love conquers all. Love is a choice, and you can love from a distance, or up close and personal. Up close and personal requires much more than love alone!

The good news is that love can also be an empowering master and a toothless monster when you open yourself to the understanding that it takes much more than love to make a grown-up relationship. It takes time, work, energy, focus and, above all, willingness!

Love takes becoming "other" wise. Beyond willingness and insight, this includes these skills:

- empathy
- communication - both listening and speaking
- anger management
- conflict management
- negotiation
- time management
- compassion
- tolerance

And more. It's not easy. I warned you. And, I also warned you that, if you and your partner are willing to do what it takes, you **can** have a grown-up relationship.

Listening is probably the most important skill you can master, when it comes to communicating fully. Learning to listen to what is said AND for what is *not* said is part of that mastery. There is only one way to do that and that is to be fully present and pay attention to all parts of the

---

[12] Kinder, Brandon, Love is Not Enough (Austin, Tx. Ghost Note Records, 2011) http://thewealthywest.bandcamp.com/

message: the words, the inflection, the tone, the pace, the volume, the facial expression and the body language. That will keep you busy!

Hearing is what your ears do. They can't help it. Listening is what you do when you give that full attention, and use your brain and heart while your ears are doing their thing. Listening it not half-hearted, or half-brained.

Communicating is not making noises in each other's direction. A communication is a message; communicating means that a message has been heard AND understood as the sender meant! That's why it takes time to be communicating. It is much more than the message. Talking may not involve communicating.

HAS TECHNOLOGY REALLY ENHANCED OUR COMMUNICATION?

I think technology is a double-edged sword: we communicate more and we fail at communicating more, too.

People react so quickly by email and text. Have you hit Send before you thought enough about the feelings you expressed, and regretted it instantly? Have you thumb-typed something in a text only to have it completely misconstrued due to lack of non-verbal cues?

It's wise to let some time pass before responding to highly emotional messages. Let the temporarily heightened feelings move away and see if that is the message you really want to send when you have cooled down. It's likely not. And, the wisdom in waiting is the damage control you need.

And having actual conversations, about important things, by text . . . never a good idea.

The same is true of speaking when you are angry. Your brain is not working effectively when you are angry. If you don't put your metaphoric hand over your very real mouth, you will blurt out in anger what you will repent and regret for longer than you care to. (If anger issues are part of your relationship, I invite you read my ebook, *Ten Absolute Essentials You Need to Keep Anger From Managing You.*)

> *Others are not experiencing or expressing your reality.*
> *They are experiencing and expressing*
> *their own reality.*

You look at life through the filter of your own experiences and learning. The only way anyone can really learn about you is to listen to you explain, explore and expand on what you are thinking and feeling. They need to listen whole-heartedly. That is the gift partners can give to each other that will make a huge difference in their level of intimacy.

There is a caveat, however: if your partner tells you something that is sensitive, tender and expressing a vulnerability, you MUST treat it as the gift it is. If, by any chance, you hear it and then use it as cannon fodder in your next big argument, you lose! Your partner will close down and shut you out. And, rightly so. *You are not trustworthy.*

That is why you need all these skills, and it is imperative that you get them. They are not picked up by osmosis alone. Glean everything you can from this book and practice, practice, practice. It will help.

Remember, developing these skills and mastering them also has great benefits for your family, your children, your career and your community involvement. Evolving does that for you!

Presence

It is not enough to be in proximity to one another. That is what many couples believe passes as being present. It does not. Proximity is great when you want to spend time in the same room, each enjoying a lone activity. Perhaps, one person is reading and the other resting. It's pleasant and you are together. That is proximity, though.

Presence is another matter. It means bringing your energy, focus and attention to the relationship and to each other. It is the active, energetic form of "being there" for your partner.

The passive version is the "S/he knows I'll be there if I'm needed." The passive version is important because it imparts trust and reliability. It does not, however, impart presence. That requires you, with all your faculties, actively being present to interact with, learn about, and share with each other in emotionally intimate ways: full physical, psychological, mental and spiritual presence. Tall order!

A polite invitation may be worded "Your presence is requested…." In a grown-up relationship, your presence is much more than requested. It is mandatory, imperative and needed. Got it?

You want your doctor to be "fully present." You don't want him or her distracted, cold, distant, aloof, or simply cordial. You don't like it when s/he is reading your file while supposedly listening to you. You want to know, and feel, that s/he is really listening, truly respectful and deeply interested in knowing you and your issues. How many times have you complained, or heard others complain, about the lack of presence in a medical deity? Isn't that what M.D. sometimes seems to stands for? It creates a standoffishness that separates the doctor from the reality of the patient. Is there any chance you might be treating each other that way at home?

> "The only way to experience the deepest levels of human experience is to be deeper in the moment in our interactions with others, fully invested in the now, with them alone."[13]
> ~ Brendon Burchard

Being fully present in each and every moment of your life is the opportunity of a lifetime. And, you've already won. You have it, or at least, you have the choice to have it. Are you making that choice? Are you making that choice when you and your partner are together?

Or, are you distracted and multi-tasking? You've likely had the experience of cooking while thinking of other things about your job. You were already working out a solution to a job problem, while trying to create a meal. You have heard the beep of two text messages which you know are from work. Then, your partner comes into the kitchen and asks a question.

As you begin to answer, you pick up a hot dish with your bare hands and the frenzy, fury and barrage begins: the pain, the blame, the string of things your mother taught you not to say. That's the result of lack of

---

[13] Burchard, Brendan. *The Charge*. Simon & Schuster, New York, 2012.

presence to any one thing. All things competing for your mind space and attention make it impossible to focus or respond without something falling through the cracks.

Back in the day in school when the roll was called, students answered "Present." There was the first lie of the day for many. They were sitting in the seat but anything but present, interested, awake, upright, energetic, and alert. They were simply there. That's not good enough for your relationship with your partner.

These days, technology has led to people believing they have superior powers of focus. They honestly believe that they can text and listen at the same time. Some even think they can drive at the same time as reading and responding to text messages with music playing, too! Really? What are they thinking? Readily-available research and case studies clearly indicate that it *is not possible.*

When you divide your attention, you are not present to anything. Think how this applies to your time with your partner. Is that enough said?

Being really present in each and every moment is challenging because you usually have your attention in the past or on the future. You may not enjoy where you are, often because you are concerned about where you are going next. Maybe you are familiar with that experience: you are on vacation and cannot enjoy sitting in the sunshine at an outside café for a couple of hours because you are focused on the guidebook and the things you have not seen yet. You simply miss the joy of the sitting, the serenity of the moment, because you are caught up in not missing something that is still in the future. And, it's a future of your own creation!

You may also spend—or more accurately, waste—a lot of precious time in your past. The only profitable time to spend there is with your therapist. Yes, it's pleasant to remember happy times and wonderful people.

That's not where the waste occurs. When you hang out in regret, blame, shame, or if-only, you'll find waste there. You know there is nothing you can do about the past except cherish the memories and not repeat the pain. Take the learning from it and move on.

Be present.

Be present to, for, and with your partner.

When you allow yourself to be fully present with your partner, s/he is new and different every day, sometimes within the hour. Your relationship (and your love-making) will stay fresh and new when you stay in the present. It's like being with a whole new person, kissing them for the very first time. Holding yourself or your mate to be as either of you were at some other time in the past means you are not open to growth. Continually bringing up things from the past causes you to miss the opportunities of the moment.

There are two common adages: "people can change" and "people never change".

Hopefully, you and your partner change. What happens to you changes you. Your responses to life change you. And, staying stuck in the past changes you because your very resistance to living in and responding to the present can make you emotionally unavailable. That cannot help but change your relationship, and not in a good way.

Be present to each other. Take some time to do this exercise together:

> Sit quietly together and softly, gently, caressingly, look into
> each other's eyes. Let your thoughts ebb away and just be pre-
> sent with each other. Stay with the moment, and with each
> moment as it unfolds. Bring your attention to your heart and

be aware of allowing love to flow from you and to you. See your partner as s/he is at this very moment.

Know that in this very moment, everything is fresh and new and anything is possible. Breathe together and focus on what you love about your partner, and rediscover it. Rest there.

You will likely find that there is great power in this exercise through stilling yourselves and taking time to be present to each other.

I can almost hear your thoughts at this moment:

"Who has time for this?"

"It will feel awkward."

"My partner won't want to do this."

"It's stupid. My partner knows I love him/her."

And, add your own. These are only resistances to being truly seen, coming from your own fears. They are not real, and they surely are not rational. The worst that can happen when you do this exercise is that you are uncomfortable, and maybe learn that you have more work to do to allow yourself to be emotionally intimate. The best that can happen is the re-igniting of that spark, the remembrance of why you love each other, and the decision that your relationship is worth these beautiful, quiet, purposeful moments together.

Be present.

Mutuality

Mutuality is for emotional grown-ups. It is based on an interest in each other as whole, complex people living in the present. When dependence or co-dependence are consistently present in a relationship, mutuality cannot be. Mutuality, then, is a defining condition for a healthy mature relationship.

No scorecards. No tallies. No tit-for-tat. No barters. Mutuality eliminates those. It requires you to be present (no surprise there), empathetic, self-aware and "other" wise. Mutuality calls you to give up the role-to-role relationship you may have unwittingly established and replace it with a soul-to-soul relationship. Soul, in this case, means your authentic self, your true self. No masks. No varnish. No pretending, either. This is what allows you to have that consistent emotional intimacy most humans long for. You can then be known, seen, heard, acknowledged, appreciated and accepted for who you really are.

When there are imbalances in mutuality between partners in a primary relationship, they can lead to significant psychological pain. This pain is elusive and hard to pin down or describe. It feels like a loss without a name: something's missing but what is it?

Mutuality in your relationship can provide you with purpose and meaning. When mutuality is lacking, it causes you to doubt yourself frequently and can certainly adversely affect your self-esteem.

In Webster's dictionary, mutuality is defined as "having the same feelings for the other; characterized by intimacy"[14] and most other dictionaries include the term "reciprocity" in the definition. Clearly, in a mutual exchange, you are affecting your partner and being affected by

---

[14] Webster's Ninth New Collegiate Dictionary, 1984

your partner. One of you extends yourself out to the other and you are also receptive to the impact your partner has on you. You influence each other, consciously or subconsciously, so there is a constant interchange responding to and affecting each other.

What is critical and crucial to having a developed sense of mutuality is that each of you appreciates the wholeness of each other. You need to be sufficiently emotionally intimate to be aware of what each other is going through. That comes through the willingness to be present and open, vulnerable and transparent with each other.

You are not in a loving relationship just to take care of each other's needs, or be the object and lucky recipient of each other's desires, moods, or frustrations.

Mutuality demands much more from you both. It requires your active interest in each other as different, complex and fascinating individuals. Remember how that was when you first met? Captivated by each other, every nuance, every difference was a delight. You valued those differences, the things that made that person unique, compelling, and attractive to you.

Without active mutuality, many couples think they know each other, and begin to take that knowing for granted. This can be both comforting, and a death knell for the love, joy and fascination you once knew. The latter is too risky to allow if you want your relationship to continue to be mutually engaging.

With empathy and that active interest in continuously learning about your partner as s/he changes in life, there is the opportunity to value and encourage the very qualities that make your partner different from you . . . and different from who they were last year.

When that empathy and concern flow in both directions—mutuality—you will each experience an intense affirmation of who you are, and a deep sense of yourselves as a committed couple. You can then relax into the relationship knowing that you each have each other's well-being as a priority.

Merging with another does not need to blur the lines and make you indistinct from each other. Far from it. There is no need to lose yourself in your partner or the relationship. That would simply deny the attractiveness of the two distinct individuals you were before meeting. Of course, as you continue through life together, you may develop similarities, and grow similar interests, but that's not a given. You may smooth off a few of each other's rough edges, even, but you can still remain individual, together.

This is an appropriate place for another word about boundaries. Clarifying, expressing and maintaining them helps you keep your autonomy in healthy ways. They are necessary for physical, mental, emotional and spiritual health and security, too. There is no question about that. Many people drop their boundaries when they fall in love. The safer you feel, the fewer boundaries you may want to mount or maintain. But, far too many folks let their boundaries with their partners disintegrate completely. Then, they wonder when they feel violated. They wonder why they feel unsafe, confused or let down. "How did we get here?" they ask.

Mutuality and empathy allow for that paradigm of safety to change in a healthy way, and for the opportunity for mutual growth and impact. Clear boundaries protect that.

What is important in mutuality is that you magnify your attunement and responsiveness to each other. You talk more, become more vulnerable and transparent with each other. You feel safe to share what is going on within you with your partner–your thoughts, feelings, fears and desires. Empathy fosters this and you can continue to deepen that safety, to become each other's safe sanctuary in the world.

You must stay present to and in touch with one another, though. Make quiet time for frequent conversations, not just about what happened in your days, but about how you felt when it happened. You can then begin to really understand how your partner sees his/her world and responds to it. There are endless possibilities for learning about each other when you set aside the time to do so.

Remember, too, when having these intimate talks, the value of removing that very destructive word from your vocabularies: *should*. When you or your partner share your insights or feelings with each other, you are opening yourself up, letting your partner see in to you. (Remember "in-to-me-see?") When you do that, perhaps exposing a tender, private insight, you are giving him/her the gift of vulnerability. It is a fragile, grand gift. It must always be treated as such. That means that you keep that insight safe. It NEVER becomes ammunition to hurt your partner with in your next angry battle!

Removing the word "should" from a conversation about feelings is imperative. When your partner makes him or herself vulnerable with you, s/he is looking for support, not for permission. The conversation might go like this:

> SHE: "I'm feeling really hurt because Martha has been ignoring me for weeks."

> HE: "You shouldn't feel like that. You know Martha."

> SHE: "Knowing Martha and knowing my feeling of being hurt are not the same thing."

> HE: "Well, you shouldn't let it get to you."

> SHE: "I need you to know that I was sharing my feeling with

you, not asking for your permission to feel it. There are no "shoulds" when it comes to feelings."

It is really important to grasp that there are no "shoulds" when it comes to feelings.

If either of you have been guilty of *shoulding* on each other, make an agreement to stop now. When you *should* on each other, you shut down the conversation and close down the safety that leads to greater intimacy. It has to be safe to share. When it isn't, you close up to protect yourself. You cannot do both things at once!

When you value the process of knowing, respecting and enhancing your own growth and that of your partner, you value the relationship. You are not consciously or unconsciously manipulating each other to get a greater sense of gratification or satisfaction while overlooking the experiences, feelings, wants and needs of your partner.

Trampled grass often never recovers.
Do not trample on your partner's vulnerabilities.
Nothing could be further from demonstrating love.

Mutuality, then, is a two-way street with no obstacles, detours or tempting parking places. It must flow openly, unobstructed. When obstructions do arise, make an agreement with your partner to use the Personal Weather Report. It is an invaluable aid for developing the mutuality that will allow you both to be and feel known, seen, heard, acknowledged, appreciated and accepted.

Choice

Choice is one of the greatest privileges—and joys—in the world, but for many folks, it is very difficult. KAIZEN FOR COUPLES invites you to open yourself to recognizing and valuing choice as a key ingredient in a healthy relationship.

You always have choice. You can:

- go or stay
- speak up or clam up
- demand or request
- ask questions or make statements
- escalate or resolve
- withhold or give
- approach or turn away
- be empathetic or callous
- be proximate or present
- pay attention or ignore
- care or brush off
- be selfish or giving
- be self-centered or engaging

There are lots of choices. And, they change with circumstances, situations, life events, and even with your mood. What would it take for you to choose the more positive in each case? What would it take for you to give your partner your best? It's your choice.

There is a lot of popular psychology that tells you what you want to hear. (That's why is it called "pop" psychology.) It becomes popular because it gives you the rationales—or excuses—to behave as your ego self most wants to behave: selfishly and in your own best interests. You can do that, sure, and you'll become part of the discouragingly—and unnecessarily large—number of people who get divorced. They "didn't get what they wanted."

Certainly, you have a reasonable expectation when you embark on a committed relationship that each of you will enjoy and benefit from being together. That's why you chose to embark. It may also be that you bought into that pop psychology, ego-driven proposition that "each of us will get our needs met." In fact, you may even be under the false impression that your partner is there to meet your needs. That's the beginning of the end right there.

Your partner is not there to meet your needs.

Darn! So what's this partnership thing all about then? What's the point?

If you are in a relationship to "get" something, you are in it for the wrong reason. You cannot fix your relationship to get a "win" out of it. This is not a game, a battle or a war.

A committed relationship gives you a partner to walk through life with, a person you can count on to go through the ups, downs and often sideways turnings in your life paths. It gives you a partner to walk with as you experience the joys, depths, confusions and growth points of life. If you are expecting something different, or tangible, you may be sorely disappointed with a grown-up relationship.

In the best case, you choose a companion who will share in figuring out the rough patches and enjoy the smooth sailing with you. You choose someone you believe can go the distance with you–and you with them.

Is this the moment when the dream of "happily ever after" becomes a cashed reality check?

Are you having an "aha" moment, as your recognize that you didn't have those criteria when you got into your relationship?

Good. This is the beginning of something much better.
Choosing real love!

Your ego wants to get a win out of everything. Your relationship is not the place to look for that. Your relationship can be, however, a real place and space where you can give and receive life, breath, movement and meaning.

You really can have a life-giving, love-enriching, grown-up
relationship...if you are willing.
It's a choice.

A word about demands, threats and ultimatums. These are power games masquerading as choices.

When one person forces another to make a choice that ultimately has just one "winner", that's "*relationship roulette*." There is a difference between boundaries and ultimatums. Boundaries are reasonable, rational lines that mark your comfort zones, your values and your beliefs. Ultimatums are the ego's desperate last-ditch attempt to get what it wants.

Unfortunately, many people believe they are being grown-up while playing these power games masquerading as choice.

> "If you don't do that for me, you're just proving that you don't love me."

> "If you don't take care of that for me, this relationship is over."

Ultimatums are examples of a toxic phenomenon called "all-or-nothing thinking." Sometimes called *splitting* when psychologists use it, "all-or-nothing thinking" is when you cannot see the grey between the opposites. It's thinking in extremes, and very rigid black and white terms.

A common example in relationships: one minute your partner is the love of your life but the split occurs in the nanosecond it takes for your partner to not do what you wanted. Now, your partner is evil incarnate, or, at a minimum, not worthy of bothering with or being with. All of a sudden, you're done, it's over. What?!

The *all* in "all-or-nothing thinking" is *all good*, or *all bad*, with no middle ground at all. That's not choice. That is a pattern that needs immediate attention in order for your relationship to survive. That kind of thinking demonstrates the "hokey-pokey relationship" I spoke of earlier.

Splitting creates constant instability in a relationship because you never know where you stand. Neither of you know where you stand. If you are the all-or-nothing thinker, you are confused, overwhelmed and often, highly emotional. You don't want to be left alone, but you don't want whatever you see as the problem, either. If you are on the receiving end of all-or-nothing thinking, you are confused, caught off-guard and possibly paralyzed by the extremity of it all. It can be crazy-making!

Do you want me or don't you? Neither of you know. One minute you are the incarnation of virtue, the next you are the incarnation of vice, and it can all happen in a moment.

"Go away but don't leave me." Crazy-making!

Do I want you or don't I?

You know you do, but you don't know what to do in the moments that you don't.

When you think like this, when your partner fails to meet your needs or frustrates you, you want him or her gone. But, you are also equally terrified of the idea of being left. No question that this leads to chaotic and unstable relationship patterns and confusing mood swings. If you find yourself or your partner often engages in splitting, see an experienced relationship therapist. It's difficult to work that out on your own. Knowledge and insight, along with better skills, will really help you.

A healthy relationship is not a battle of wins and wills. Neither is it about ego-gratification. It's about the Relational Gifts of honesty, safety, trust, respect and reliability. Those are what gives life to a healthy relationship, and sustains it.

Remember, much as you might want it to be different, your partner is not there to meet your needs, nor satisfy your ego. You're a grown-up—or, at least, an adult—and meeting your needs is your job!

Speaking of Grown-up or Adult…

Adult is just a stage of physical and mental growth. After baby, toddler, pre-schooler, school-age, high-school, and perhaps college, you magically arrive at adult. Problem is, there are many more adults in the world than grown-ups! **Grown-ups are people who have come to understand that there is no one to blame for their thoughts, actions, situations, circumstances, lives or feelings. They accept responsibility and accountability for them themselves.**

Why? Because they have choice!

Parents meet the needs of their children until the children can meet their own needs. Healthy relationships happen between healthy people who have become grown-ups: they are not looking for someone else to meet their needs. They don't want to have to parent their partners. They want relationships of mutuality!

In that pop psychology I mentioned, you'll find the gamut of books, programs, retreats and talk show hosts—even some counselors or relationship coaches—telling you that you *should*, indeed, be able to look to your partner to meet your needs. And, if s/he won't, if s/he withholds that from you, there is no love there. **They are right about one thing: there is no love there, but it's not love *between* the partners that is missing. It is the *self-love of* the partners that is absent.**

When you love yourself, you take care of yourself. You know you matter and you treat yourself as though you do. You don't need someone else to do that for you. Grown-ups take care of themselves. They treat themselves with those same Relational Gifts: honesty, safety, trust, respect and reliability. If you are having difficulty in your relationship, look at yourself first. Are you giving yourself those gifts? If not, you will not have them to give.

> *True partnership is desirable.*
> *Mutuality is the key ingredient.*
>
> *Even when things are difficult, mutuality sustains you as a team both willing and able to meet challenges together.*

It's true that, under everything, every relationship is plagued with the inevitable struggle of each partner to manage his or her ego. The ego is a demanding, self-preserving auto-program that wants everything its own way, on its own terms. Gimme, gimme, gimme!

The ego wants to tell the story, and oh, how it really wants a juicy story to tell! You know that because it is your ego that goes running to your friend looking for sympathy, empathy, understanding and an ally when your partner just doesn't meet your needs. You want someone to understand—and affirm—that you are hard done by and deserving of so much more. You want someone to take your side—and your hand. It's the ego that drives you to spill your guts to your friends—or total strangers. Don't do that.

*Remember, your conversations about your relationship
belong only between you and your partner, and,
if you are wise, also with your therapist.*

A good therapist is a highly-trained "neutral" who doesn't take sides or create allegiances. S/he will help you find the insights, solutions and stamina to make positive changes in yourself and your contributions to your relationship. S/he will help you sort out your real feelings, thoughts, wants and needs and clarify your best next steps. Working with you and your partner, s/he can lead you to new levels of clarity, understanding, love, trust and intimacy, and to establish effective skills to communicate and manage conflict.

A healthy, thriving relationship means you understand what it means to be a good diving buddy.

It's easy to enjoy a great day of scuba diving with and apart from your partner. You enjoy the depths, and surface every now and again to tell each other what you've seen and what they might enjoy seeing. You share the experience along with the exuberance, excitement and enjoyment.

But, diving along together, all of a sudden, one partner's tank is stripped away and s/he is left floundering. The only way to get to the surface is by sharing one tank of air. Even though it is difficult, exhausting, even terrifying, you both suffer as you make your way to safety. That's mutuality AND choice. It builds trust and intimacy.

You both have to learn to take smaller breaths sometimes. You may not get all the oxygen you want, but it will be all you need to survive. You do this so that the relationship can survive. When one demands all the air, there is a vacuum created for the other. That's when the ego wants it all and it gets demanding. There is no oxygen for the other to survive. That's not partnership.

A healthy, mutual relationship is like scuba diving with one tank of air. The only way to stay alive is to not panic, share the tank and get back to the surface safely—together. Ditching your partner to satisfy your ego's need to be right is not the answer. You have to have the skills and willingness to work together to get to the surface again. It's a risky business, and it takes practice along with that skill and willingness. But, that's the commitment you made to each other.

If your real promise was to bail at the first, second or tenth sign of struggle, you need to own that. If you really are in it to experience what true loving really is, you'll go through the pain and difficulties of sharing a tank when you need to. It's a choice!

As a Grown-up, choosing has to be done over and over again.

The initial choice that got you into a relationship may have been made in a haze of pheromones and heady promises of undying love through whatever may come. The real choices show up in the difficult times and they become clear when oxygen becomes limited.

Will you grab that tank and run because you "deserve" to have it all? Will you sacrifice the tank and give up on yourself? Or, will you share the tank, take smaller breaths, and get you both—and your relationship—to the surface safely? And given the same choices, would your partner do the same?

I was working with a couple who were divorcing. They came to me to mediate an equitable parenting plan which would be part of their marital settlement document. Jane was a stay-at-home mom who previously had a high-level career. James was a well-respected medical professional, making significant contributions to his profession. They had been living separately for a year, and wanted to make this formal parenting plan to reduce conflicts and provide some stability to themselves and the children.

The problem was that Jane thought James was not a sufficiently present dad to have the children half of the time. While uncovering her reasons for this, it came to light that Jane spent her life taking care of the children and liked it that way, but she defined taking care of the children as keeping them entertained. James did not want to be an entertainer. He thought that the children had to be able to entertain themselves some of the time because they were already nine and twelve years old. He thought the children needed to become independent enough to not need a parent to be engaged with them every moment.

This set up a conflict between a verdict and a choice. Jane rendered a verdict that James was inadequate as a custodial parent because he didn't make the choices she thought he *should* make when he had the children. Her verdict was that he had to be hyper-adequate to be deemed minimally acceptable to her as a custodial parent. Nothing less than full engagement with his kids at all times was acceptable.

Further, she had a strong underlying belief that James only wanted fifty-percent custody because he "wanted to hurt her." She was sure that he only wanted the kids so that she could not have them. Further, she believed he only wanted equally shared custody to save in child support payments.

Throughout their marriage, Jane had stayed home and James had provided. That was the status quo. Jane decided that she no longer wanted to live with or be married to James, however, she wanted everything else to continue as it had been. Strangely, she chose not to see that her choice to end the marriage was also the end of life as she had become accustomed to it!

She saw no reason why she could not still be the full-time parent with James having only twenty-five percent custody, and that conferred begrudgingly by her. Why *should* she change? Her verdict was in: she was the better parent and James just wanted the kids to be mean and cheap. It didn't seem to me that that was the case.

Jane had her verdict. Because the split was so new and Jane had been withholding the kids from James, he could not overcome Jane's verdict of the past life together. She prevented him from creating new patterns of behavior with the children. She insisted that his parenting was inferior. It was not possible for her to see a new situation—which she chose to create—and allow for change to occur. She could have chosen to see things differently and negotiate new choices. These did not suit her purposes for keeping her life the same as always except for the exclusion of her husband from her life.

Can you un-choose a choice?

Good question. You cannot un-choose a choice, but you *can* re-choose. You can make another choice. You can accommodate poor choices by working things out in the present. You can choose differently in the present moment and proceed from the new choice. That's always an option, if you open yourself to it.

Choices are defining moments. The question before you in each moment is:

> *"How do we make this journey together honest, respectful, trusting and loving today?"*

You actually don't marry for life. You re-choose each other every day. Good relationships can't just be summed up in a single trite sentence. You cannot come up with a story that always makes you a winner. You have to choose to live life each day as it comes.

Life can be done through kaizen: small positive choices consistently made and sustained. A story cannot be. We like stories to sum things up, prove points, and create lessons. When you have a story about your relationship, it is already in the past. You've tried to sum it up. How can you sum up something that is constantly growing and evolving?

> *Choose life, not stories. You want what is real,*
> *not just a story to tell your friends or family.*

Real love is whole-hearted: it is through acceptance, gratitude, trust and surrender that we go all-in. Life is where you discover, learn and grow love. It's much more *motion* than *emotion!* It is in that motion that you demonstrate who you are by what you do. That's real. Words are not.

Choose each other. Choose the relationship and act on that choice every day.

 I Choose YOU!

For your relationship to have a healthy, vital life, you must be able to say those words, no matter what the mood, event or situation,

"I Choose You."

If you cannot or will not say this, your relationship is already in trouble and in need of immediate help. There will be some, if not many, days when you have to back up and take the long view to allow yourself to say it. Up close and personal at some moments, it might be hard to spit out. That's why this is a critical chapter to embrace and implement.

Even if your relationship is uncomfortable right now, maybe even downright miserable, most relationships can be reconstructed into something much better than either partner thought possible. It takes commitment, ability and willingness on each partner's part, though, and that's where the rubber hits the road.

Do you want to do the work, or do you want to go out and repeat your patterns with another partner and end up in the same place, time and again? That's what happens, and you already likely know that is true.

Unfolding love is in the willingness to make the "heart" choices and follow them up with the hard choices. Those are the ones where you are feeling the pinch of old patterns and the clash of opposing values and visions, and choose to keep on walking together. You are forging something amazing, even when it sometimes feels agonizing. It's definitely worth it.

To not choose is still a choice.

Toro and Sonia came to a Relationship Insights class one evening. This small weekly class helps people understand they are not alone in their relationship difficulties and provides an opportunity to talk about what's going on.

Toro admitted that he had a few beers every night just as the kids were going to bed. But, he was always home, not out carousing with friends. He was clear that he was, therefore, a good husband. Sonia knew she could count on him to be at home, and she *should* be grateful for that.

Sonia was fed up and feeling alone. Although Toro was there, in proximity every night, he certainly wasn't there fully present and willing to partner. She had no one to talk with and certainly no one to solve problems or make plans with. Toro could not see his drinking as his way of withdrawing from any possibilities for problem-solving conversations with Sonia.

As they attended class over the weeks, Toro and Sonia realized that they had drifted into an unwritten agreement: I'll stay home and you stay quiet. Really, it was a stand-off. Sonia had been the first to make a move. She clarified her boundaries and expressed them clearly. She chose to honor her need to feel safe, secure, and happy. For this to happen, she needed Toro to:

1. Stop drinking and engage with her as real partners do.
   OR
2. Move out and do what he liked.

Toro did not want to leave his home, his wife or his children. He loved them. So, he chose option one. He went to AA and they came to class together. Sonia's clear boundaries gave Toro a way to demonstrate what really mattered to him. Is that what you need to do, too?

Wake up and recognize that, with every word and action, you are making a choice. Recognize any of these poor choices?

- You sweep issues under the rug or nag about them until you "win".
- You talk to friends about your relationship issues rather than talk with your partner.
- You are pretending to be available (proximate) instead of being emotionally available (present.)
- You think your relationship issues would all go away if only your partner would change.
- You escape from reality by choosing alcohol, drugs, video games, gambling or working out instead of your partner.
- You tell yourself a good story filled with reasons and justifications for your behavior, instead of facing the reality.
- You think you are putting on a good show in order to stay together "for the sake of the children." (P.S. That's impossible!)
- You try to justify your anger by making it your partner's fault.
- You hide behind being a good provider while being a lousy partner.
- You sabotage your relationship by not doing things you promised to do.

- You tell your partner what to do while failing to do it yourself.
- You have expectations of your partner and withhold your attention or affection if those expectations are not met.
- You negate your partner's feelings and tell him or her how s/he *should* feel.
- You vigorously defend your right to behave as you do while vehemently denying your partner's rights.
- You alienate your partner by creating allegiances with friends and family by discussing your relationship with them.
- You use your children as confidantes, and burden them with emotional and relationship issues. It is inappropriate for them to hear or be informed from either of you about adult issues.
- You go to church and put on a good show and return home and behave in unloving ways.
- You say better but don't do better.

Are some of these choices that you are making? I promise, all they will do is keep you miserable, mad and marginalized in your relationship, and do the same for your partner.

Have you:

- Looked in the mirror and noticed your eyes have gone dead? The twinkle is gone, or at least dulled considerably?
- Looked at your partner and found there is nothing that looks like love looking back at you?

These are two of many possible undesirable results of making choices like those above.

You CAN choose differently.

Make small positive choices to move in these directions:

- Begin to see your partner *as* a partner.
- Remember that you can't and don't *fix* feelings, you *listen* to them.
- Recognize that you affect each other by the choices you make, regardless of why you make them.
- Take responsibility for your words and actions, no matter how anyone else—including your partner—is behaving.
- Become a little more open with how you are feeling rather than protecting and defending yourself.
- Recognize that what you do and say in your relationship makes a difference.
- Acknowledge when you are in pain and feeling lonely, even when you may be choosing to push your partner away.
- Take time to listen to your partner.
- Acknowledge that you teach your children by what you *do*—no matter what you say to them.
- Demonstrate respect for yourself and your partner.
- See your partner's struggle and reach out to listen.
- Acknowledge problems and focus on solutions.
- Let old hurts disappear from your conversations.
- Let down your guard and let your partner see your inner world of hopes, dreams, pains and desires.
- Release your judgment about how things *should* be and work with what *is*.
- Notice when you are becoming defensive and flip your internal switch to becoming curious about your partner instead.
- Plan something you think your partner will enjoy.
- Give your partner the gift of your time and attention.

- Relax together and take a break from the pressures of life. (Those pressures will still be there if you want to go back and pick them up.)
- Consciously create time to just be together, without plans or agendas. Just be present to each other, and interested in each other.
- Choose to remember what you love about your partner and share it him or her.
- Focus on what is good in your relationship and let it expand.
- Become more compassionate with yourself and your partner. You're both human and life can be painful, difficult and complicated.
- Recognize the work you have to do on yourself rather than focusing on the work you think your partner *should* do.
- Engage your partner in remembering the times you really "worked" as a couple and the joy and pleasure it brought. Then, agree to move towards creating it again.
- Learn to tell your truth in ways that are kind and honest at the same time.
- Invite your partner to go with you to get new insights and wise guidance to create more loving ways of interacting and doing life together.
- Share your gratitude for your partner still being with you even though things may have become sticky, muddy, trying or ugly at times.
- Commit to having the tough conversations and not denying the need for them.
- Recognize that you have the power to create a more positive, loving future and commit to that direction.
- Create a safe place where you can both talk about your fears, hurts, struggles and disappointments without blame.

- Recognize that there is never a "good time" to talk about difficult things and make a determined effort to talk about them as they come up. No more piles under carpets!
- Embrace a positive regard for your partner, no matter what s/he has done, said, not done or not said earlier.
- Give up defensiveness.
- Make time and pay attention to sharing your Personal Weather Reports and respond only with curiosity to learn more about your partner.
- Hold your partner's hand more.
- Gaze into your partner's eyes more.
- Give, share and find love within yourself once again.

Demonstrate the spirit of "I Choose You" in all your thoughts, words and actions.

You have choice. You make choices every moment that you're breathing. Choose wisely.

The one person you think you know the best in all the world may still be a wonderful mystery to you and the source of great joy, love and companionship for a lifetime. You'll never know unless you embrace the spirit of "I Choose You."

Lasting Love REQUIRES much more than FOND GAZES warm embraces & GOOD INTENTIONS IT is only PRESENT when BOTH OF YOU WITHOUT RESERVATION CAN SAY & WITH TRUST, HONESTY & RESPECT, I CHOOSE YOU NO MATTER THE CIRCUMSTANCES.

- Rhoberta Shaler, PhD, The Relationship Help Doctor   www.ForRelationshipHelp.com

CHAPTER 11

Gently Unfolding Truth, Trust & Intimacy

You want to be known, seen, heard, acknowledged, appreciated and accepted—especially by the person you love the most and want to grow old with. You want your partner to have that depth and freedom, too. Truth, trust and intimacy are not just natural uprisings as a result of spending time in proximity to one another.

It's not how many years you spend together.
It's how you spend your years.

Grown-up relationships are built on KAIZEN FOR COUPLES principles, skills and insights. And now, when you consciously practice them daily, they gently lead you to unfold truth, trust and intimacy together.

If you have *slowly* read this entire book, you have the basis you need. Just in case you may have cheated yourself of fully understanding the processes by skipping around or just choosing chapters you are drawn to, I invite you to read the book again from front to back.

The process and system of KAIZEN FOR COUPLES is laid out for you in a progressive order of things to learn, reflect on and practice. You now have so many more tools for becoming self-aware and "other" wise. Your confidence, comfort and capacity to see through, think through and work through things that arise between you will have grown. Your ability to discuss issues, solve problems, and appreciate each other in the process will have grown exponentially. You will have gently unfolded more love, trust and intimacy than you may have thought possible.

What is a Grown-up Relationship?

To be a grown-up you know that there is nothing or no one to blame for your current thoughts, feelings, actions and desires. You also take responsibility and are accountable for what you create and the consequences, too. The real definition of your grown-up relationship will be the one that you create for yourself. Only you know what the ultimate relationship for you would be.

I want to encourage you to think bigger than you possibly have in order to reach for that ultimate definition. I can guarantee you that your definition will grow as you do. The more inner work you do, the more time you spend in meaningful conversation with your partner, the more you will realize what is possible for you both.

Throughout this book, you have read many of the components of a grown-up relationship. First, it must be based on having the Relational Gifts to give:

- Honesty
- Safety
- Trust
- Respect
- Reliability

You'll remember from that chapter that you have to do your own work first. You have to give those gifts to yourself before you have them to offer to your partner. That's where doing your own work precedes your partner work.

In order to give the Relational Gifts to yourself, you have to know and live in alignment with your:

- Values
- Vision
- Beliefs
- Purposes

This again calls for you to work on yourself. You may often become impatient with the need to do that. Can't we just solve these problems between us and make everything better? Sure, you can work on an issue and that may help. Underneath every issue, however, are two people. If those two people don't know who they are, what they stand for, what they want and where they are going as individuals, how can they possibly give their best to their partner and the relationship?

You may have a big, pressing desire to fix the relationship, or your partner. That's where the problems lie. Yes, sometimes you really believe that all would be well if your partner just changed. I know that. You know that. However, you also now know from reading this book that that is not the path to a grown-up relationship!

A grown-up relationship offers you both the freedom, the depth, the understanding, the certainty that you are truly known, and accepted whole-heartedly by that one very special person in your life. It provides the springboard from which each of you can launch your most effective, productive, empowered life. You know you have someone in your corner who won't run from difficult conversations, won't judge or dismiss your feelings, thoughts, wants or needs, and will always be your confidant, coach and cheerleader. A grown-up!

CHAPTER 12

The Ten "Us-sentials"

t's complicated. You get together and you are still a "you," but there is another entity that is an "us." The balance between the "us" and the "you" require careful consideration daily. Yes, daily.

Relationships are not perfect and feelings are not facts. Those are two important things to keep in mind. Relationships are organic and dynamic, always changing, just like feelings.

It's a big risk to put your relationship on autopilot and wake up somewhere you had no intention of going. That happens to a lot of couples and you don't have to be among them.

If you go on autopilot, your partner may have grown while you were absent and unavailable. That's why I encourage you to practice KAIZEN FOR COUPLES daily: taking small, consistent, positive steps.

Feelings are not facts. Some feelings are fleeting and temporary. Some are renewed and maintained by your values, your thoughts, and conscious choices, like love. You may not actually feel love, loving or loved in the moment, but you can choose love over the anger or upset you may feel in the moment. When you choose love, your perspective and approach changes.

I'm sharing the Ten "Us-sentials" with you to give you a glimpse into the results you can experience by committing to KAIZEN FOR COUPLES principles and processes, together. These are covered in depth in the KAIZEN FOR COUPLES Weekends and the KAIZEN FOR COUPLES Relationars™. Consider those once you have begun to see the value of using what you've found in this book. You are worth it.

KAIZEN FOR COUPLES offers you the small, positive steps you can take now to discover, uncover, or recover the love you once felt sure you knew.

No matter what has gone before, with these steps, willingness and patience, you can take this miraculous journey towards each other once again.

You can take it together consciously, purposefully and intentionally. This is the greatest gift you can give yourself, and give to each other.

The Ten "Us-sentials"

1. I am not perfect. You are not perfect. Our relationship is not perfect.

2. Mutuality is a must. "We" is always a consideration over "I."

3. Each of us must be consciously committed to the journey of "us."

4. Surrender expectations and outcomes.

5.. Give up the need to be right.

6. We are partners to each other, not parents.

7. Embrace giving to, listening to and engaging with each other.

8. Make a mutual commitment to the RelationSteps™.

9. Know that the Personal Weather Report is more important than the nightly news.

10. Demonstrate that "you matter" daily, individually and as a couple.

© Rhoberta Shaler, 2014

Live. Love. Laugh. Embrace. Encourage. Empower.

Keep learning. Walk on . . . together.

♥ About Rhoberta Shaler

Rhoberta Shaler, PhD, The Relationship Help Doctor, has been working with people struggling with life, death and relationship for over thirty years in the United States and Canada. She has brought hope, comfort, strength and success to countless people who honestly believed it was impossible. Through that experience, she developed tools and strategies her clients can master to sustain their relationship progress, gently unfolding truth, trust and intimacy.

When she won a cross-Canada competition to be principal of a private school for children and at-risk teens many years ago, she became more acutely aware of the intricacies and complexities of family dynamics. As she walked, wept, and worked with people in pain, she observed firsthand the breakdown of trust, honesty, respect and safety, and its impact on couples and their children. She dedicated herself to finding and sharing new approaches to relationship that lead to the healing, wholeness, and happiness that every family deserves.

Dr. Shaler wrote *Kaizen for Couples* to walk with you.

❤️ You Can Get Relationship Help Right Away

You can participate in Dr. Rhoberta Shaler's ongoing classes, teleclasses, webinars, weekends, and of course, private relationship sessions in-person at **The Optimize Center** in Escondido, CA and online via Skype® and Google Hangouts®.

For complete details about the KAIZEN FOR COUPLES introductory and intensive programs & retreats, visit www.KaizenForCouples.com

Find free resources and much more information about how to create—and keep—your great relationships at:

www.RelationshipHelpDoctor.com

- Subscribe to free Tips for Relationships – Twice a month email newsletter.
- Take her free online **Relationship Checklist**
- Take her free online **Passive-Aggressive Checklist**
- Find all of Dr. Shaler's other books and ebooks to purchase online.
- Follow on The Relationship Help Doctor on Facebook, Twitter, LinkedIn, and Pinterest.

CPSIA information can be obtained at www.ICGtesting.com
Printed in the USA
BVOW10s1644080615

403009BV00020B/130/P